HOW TO SURVIVE WHEN THE GRID GOES DOWN

HOW TO SURVIVE WHEN THE GRID GOES DOWN

THE ULTIMATE GRID-DOWN SURVIVAL GUIDE FOR THRIVING IN A WORLD WITHOUT POWER

SELF-SUFFICIENT LIVING
BOOK 2

ANTHONY BENNETT

Book Bound
STUDIOS

Copyright © 2024 by Anthony Bennett

All rights reserved. No part of this book may be reproduced, stored in a retrieval system, or transmitted in any form or by any means, electronic, mechanical, photocopying, recording, or otherwise, without the prior written permission of the publisher, Book Bound Studios.

The information contained in this book is based on the author's personal experiences and research. While every effort has been made to ensure the accuracy of the information presented, the author and publisher cannot be held responsible for any errors or omissions.

This book is intended for general informational purposes only and is not a substitute for professional medical, legal, or financial advice. If you have specific questions about any medical, legal, or financial matters, you should consult with a qualified healthcare professional, attorney, or financial advisor.

Book Bound Studios is not affiliated with any product or vendor mentioned in this book. The views expressed in this book are those of the author and do not necessarily reflect the views of Book Bound Studios.

This book is dedicated to humanity's resilient spirit and to all those who seek to safeguard their future against uncertainty. To the families who prioritize preparedness, the individuals who strive for self-sufficiency, and the communities that come together in times of need, may this guide empower you to face any challenge with confidence and courage. Let it be a beacon of knowledge and hope, illuminating the path to resilience and readiness in a world where the only constant is change.

Survival can be summed up in three words — never give up. That's the heart of it really. Just keep trying.

— BEAR GRYLLS

CONTENTS

Introduction to Grid Down Survival   xiii

1. WATER PROCUREMENT AND PURIFICATION   1
   Finding Water Sources   1
   Methods of Water Purification   3
   Storing and Conserving Water   5
   Recognizing and Avoiding Contaminated Water   7
   Rainwater Collection Techniques   9
   Chapter Summary   11

2. FOOD ACQUISITION AND STORAGE   13
   Hunting and Trapping for Food   13
   Foraging for Edible Plants   15
   Preserving Food Without Electricity   17
   Creating a Survival Garden   19
   Livestock and Animal Husbandry Basics   20
   Chapter Summary   22

3. SHELTER AND SECURITY   25
   Choosing a Safe Location   25
   Building Temporary Shelters   27
   Constructing Long-Term Habitats   29
   Home Fortification Techniques   31
   Security Measures and Perimeter Defense   33
   Fire Safety and Management   35
   Chapter Summary   37

4. HEALTH AND FIRST AID   39
   Basic First Aid Skills   39
   Handling Common Injuries and Illnesses   41
   Natural Remedies and Alternative Medicines   44
   Maintaining Hygiene and Sanitation   45

Preventing and Treating Waterborne Diseases — 46
Mental Health and Coping Mechanisms — 48
Chapter Summary — 50

5. ENERGY AND POWER ALTERNATIVES — 53
Solar Power Basics — 53
Wind Energy Fundamentals — 55
Hydro Power Options — 57
Manual Power Generation Techniques — 58
Battery Storage and Management — 60
Creating a Renewable Energy Plan — 62
Chapter Summary — 65

6. COMMUNICATION AND NAVIGATION — 67
Basic Signaling Techniques — 67
Using Radios for Communication — 69
Navigating Without GPS — 71
Map Reading and Land Navigation — 73
Creating and Using Codes — 75
Maintaining Operational Security — 76
Chapter Summary — 78

7. SURVIVAL GEAR AND TOOLS — 81
Essential Survival Gear — 81
Choosing and Maintaining Tools — 83
DIY Survival Tools — 85
Multi-Use Items for Survival — 87
Packaging and Transporting Gear — 89
Innovative Uses for Common Items — 91
Chapter Summary — 93

8. SELF-DEFENSE AND TACTICAL TRAINING — 95
Basic Self-Defense Techniques — 95
Firearms Training and Safety — 97
Improvised Weapons and Tools — 99
Tactical Movement and Camouflage — 100
Situational Awareness and Threat Assessment — 101
Building a Survival Team — 104
Chapter Summary — 106

9. PSYCHOLOGICAL PREPAREDNESS AND
   LEADERSHIP   109
   Mental Resilience in Survival Situations   109
   Effective Leadership and Team Dynamics   111
   Conflict Resolution and Negotiation   114
   Stress Management Techniques   115
   Building Morale and Maintaining Hope   117
   Training and Preparing Your Mind for Survival   119
   Chapter Summary   122

10. COMMUNITY BUILDING AND
    NETWORKING   125
    Forming and Strengthening Community Ties   125
    Bartering and Trade Skills   127
    Collaborative Survival Strategies   129
    Creating Mutual Aid Networks   131
    Legal and Ethical Considerations   134
    Chapter Summary   136

11. LONG-TERM SUSTAINABILITY AND SELF-
    SUFFICIENCY   139
    Sustainable Agriculture and Permaculture   139
    Waste Management and Recycling   142
    Building and Maintaining Infrastructure   144
    Education and Skill Sharing for Self-
    Sufficiency   146
    Chapter Summary   148

12. ADAPTING TO A NEW WORLD   149
    Embracing Change and Overcoming
    Challenges   149
    Innovative Problem Solving   151
    The Role of Technology in a Post-Grid World   153
    Preserving Knowledge and Culture   155
    Environmental Stewardship   157
    Chapter Summary   159

    The Path Forward   161

Your Feedback Matters 173
About the Author 175

INTRODUCTION TO GRID DOWN SURVIVAL

Understanding the Grid and Its Importance

In the modern world, the grid is an intricate web of electrical lines, substations, transformers, and power stations working harmoniously to deliver electricity to our homes, businesses, and institutions. This network is the backbone of contemporary society, powering everything from the smallest household appliances to the largest industrial machines. The importance of the grid cannot be overstated; it is the lifeline that fuels our daily operations, communications, healthcare, and entertainment. Without it, the societal structure as we know it would grind to a halt, literally and figuratively plunging us into darkness.

The grid's role extends beyond mere convenience. It supports critical infrastructure, including water purification

Introduction to Grid Down Survival

systems, hospitals, emergency services, and transportation networks. These systems rely on a continuous electricity supply to function effectively and ensure public safety. In the event of a grid failure, the immediate impact would be felt across all sectors of society, highlighting the grid's central role in maintaining the rhythm of our daily lives.

Moreover, the grid represents human ingenuity, representing decades of technological advancement and innovation. It is a complex, interconnected system designed to meet the growing demands of an increasingly digital and electrified world. However, this complexity also makes the grid vulnerable to various threats, from natural disasters to cyber-attacks. Understanding these vulnerabilities is crucial for preparing for and mitigating the effects of grid failures.

In essence, the grid is more than just a network of cables and power stations; it is the foundation of modern civilization. Its importance cannot be understated: serving as a conduit for electricity and a critical support system for every facet of contemporary life. As we move forward, the grid's resilience and reliability will become even more critical, underscoring the need for continued investment in infrastructure and innovation to safeguard this indispensable asset.

Potential Causes for Grid Failures

The stability and functionality of the grid are paramount to our daily lives. The grid powers everything from the smallest household appliances to the largest industrial machines. However, this complex and interconnected system is not impervious to failure. Several potential causes can lead to widespread grid failures, each with unique challenges and implications. Understanding these causes is the first step in preparing for and mitigating the impacts of a grid-down scenario.

One of the most common causes of grid failure is natural disasters. Events such as hurricanes, earthquakes, floods, and severe storms can wreak havoc on the infrastructure that supports the grid. Power lines can be downed, substations flooded, and generation facilities damaged, leading to widespread outages. The severity of these disasters can vary greatly, but their capacity to disrupt the grid is undeniable.

Another significant threat to the grid comes from human-made causes, including cyber-attacks and physical sabotage. As our grid becomes increasingly digital and interconnected, the potential for cyber-attacks that could disrupt operations grows. Hackers could target anything from power generation facilities to distribution networks, causing widespread outages. Similarly, physical attacks on key infrastructure points could lead to significant disruptions. These threats highlight the importance of robust security measures to protect the grid from malicious actors.

Electromagnetic pulses (EMPs), whether from a solar flare or a man-made weapon, represent another potential cause of grid failure. An EMP could severely damage or destroy electrical and electronic equipment, leading to immediate and widespread grid failure. The likelihood of such an event is debated among experts, but the potential impact is significant enough to warrant consideration in any discussion on grid resilience.

Aging infrastructure also poses a significant risk to the grid's stability. Many of the grid's components, including power lines, transformers, and generation facilities, are decades old and nearing the end of their designed lifespan. Without proper maintenance, upgrades, and replacements, these components are more susceptible to failure, which could lead to localized or even widespread outages.

Lastly, the increasing demand for electricity, coupled with the shift towards renewable energy sources, presents both challenges and opportunities for the grid. While renewable energy sources such as wind and solar power offer cleaner alternatives to fossil fuels, they also introduce variability and unpredictability into the grid. Balancing supply and demand becomes more complex, requiring advanced technologies and management strategies to ensure stability.

In summary, the potential causes for grid failures vary, ranging from natural disasters and human-made attacks to aging infrastructure and the challenges of integrating renewable energy sources. Each of these causes presents unique challenges that require careful consideration and preparation. As we move forward, understanding these potential causes and working to mitigate their impacts will be crucial in ensuring the resilience and reliability of the grid.

Immediate Effects of a Grid-Down Scenario

Understanding the immediate effects of a grid-down scenario is crucial for anyone concerned about their ability to survive and thrive in the face of such a crisis. When the power grid fails, the repercussions are swift and far-reaching, affecting every aspect of modern life. This section delves into these immediate effects, providing a comprehensive overview to help you prepare and respond effectively.

Firstly, the loss of electricity halts the operation of essential services. Water treatment plants, for instance, rely heavily on electricity to purify and pump water to homes and businesses. Without power, the water supply quickly becomes unsafe for consumption, leading to a critical need for alternative potable water sources. Similarly, the cessation of sewage treatment facilities can result in sanitation issues, posing severe health risks.

Communication networks are another casualty of power grid failures. Cell towers, internet routers, and landline systems depend on electricity. The loss of these services disrupts the flow of information, making it challenging to obtain updates on the crisis or communicate with loved ones and emergency services. This lack of communication can exacerbate confusion and panic in the initial stages of a grid-down event.

The immediate effects on healthcare facilities can be particularly dire. Hospitals and clinics rely on power for life-saving equipment, refrigeration of medicines and vaccines,

Introduction to Grid Down Survival

and lighting for surgeries and patient care. Backup generators may provide temporary relief, but these are short-term solutions and are dependent on fuel supplies that may quickly dwindle.

Transportation systems also grind to a halt as traffic lights go out, fuel pumps at gas stations cease to operate, and public transportation systems stop running. This not only hampers evacuation efforts but also impedes the delivery of essential goods, including food and medical supplies. The resulting shortages can lead to panic buying and hoarding, further depleting available resources.

Food preservation and safety become immediate concerns as well. Refrigerators and freezers no longer function, leading to the spoilage of perishable items. This not only wastes food resources but also increases the risk of foodborne illnesses. The disruption in the food supply chain exacerbates this issue, as grocery stores are unable to restock their shelves due to transportation and communication breakdowns.

Lastly, the psychological impact of a grid-down scenario cannot be underestimated. The sudden loss of modern conveniences, coupled with the uncertainty and potential for societal breakdown, can lead to significant stress and anxiety. The fear of the unknown, along with concerns for personal safety and the well-being of loved ones, can have profound effects on mental health.

In summary, the immediate effects of a grid-down scenario are multifaceted and severe, impacting water and food supply, healthcare, communication, transportation, and psychological well-being. Understanding these impacts is the first step in preparing for and mitigating the consequences of such events, ensuring that you and your loved ones can navigate the challenges.

Long-Term Implications of Living Off-Grid

In the aftermath of a grid-down scenario, the immediate effects, such as loss of electricity, communication, and essential utilities, give way to a more profound and enduring challenge: adapting to a life off-grid. This transition, while daunting, is manageable. It requires a comprehensive understanding of the long-term implications of living without the conveniences and support systems that have become integral to modern life.

Living off-grid, by necessity, fosters a deep connection with the natural environment. This connection is not merely philosophical but practical. Water sourcing, for instance, has become a daily concern. Without access to municipal water supplies, individuals must rely on natural sources such as rivers, lakes, or rainwater collection systems. This requires knowledge of water purification techniques and an understanding of sustainable water usage to avoid depleting local resources.

Food security is another critical aspect. The reliance on grocery stores and food supply chains is replaced by self-

Introduction to Grid Down Survival

sufficiency through gardening, foraging, hunting, and fishing. This shift necessitates learning about crop rotation, soil health, seasonal planting, and food preservation for leaner times. Moreover, it underscores the importance of community and cooperation, as sharing knowledge and resources can significantly enhance survival prospects.

Energy production and management become central to off-grid living. Solar panels, wind turbines, and hydroelectric systems can provide renewable energy, but their implementation requires technical knowledge and upfront investment. Energy conservation has become a daily practice, as resources are finite and must be managed judiciously.

Healthcare, too, transforms. Without immediate access to hospitals and pharmacies, basic medical knowledge becomes invaluable. Herbal medicine, first aid, and preventative care take on new significance, emphasizing the need for education and preparedness in these areas.

The psychological impact of this transition cannot be understated. The shift from a life of convenience to self-reliance requires mental resilience and adaptability. The sense of community becomes more pronounced as individuals rely on each other for support, knowledge, and companionship in ways that were previously taken for granted.

In conclusion, the long-term implications of living off-grid extend far beyond the initial loss of utilities and conveniences. They touch every aspect of daily life, from water and food to energy, healthcare, and community.

Adapting to this new reality requires practical skills and knowledge and a profound shift in mindset. While challenging, it is a journey that can lead to a deeper understanding of self-reliance, sustainability, and the importance of community.

1
WATER PROCUREMENT AND PURIFICATION

Finding Water Sources

In a grid-down scenario, finding reliable water sources becomes a paramount concern for survival. Whether urban or rural, the landscape around you holds various potential water sources, but knowing where to look and how to access these sources safely is crucial. This section delves into practical strategies for locating water in environments that may initially seem devoid of this essential resource.

Natural water sources include rivers, streams, lakes, and ponds. These are often the most visible and accessible sources. However, their water quality can vary significantly depending on the surrounding environment and upstream activities. When approaching natural water sources, it's important to assess the area for signs of contamination, such as discolored water, unnatural odors, or dead wildlife. In wilderness areas, moving water, such as streams and rivers, is generally preferable to stagnant water, as it is less likely to harbor pathogens and parasites.

Rainwater is a relatively clean water source, making it ideal for collection and use. Setting up a rainwater collection system can be as simple as positioning clean containers outside during rainfall. Tarps or plastic sheets can funnel rainwater into containers for more efficient collection. Ensuring the collection surfaces and containers are clean is essential to avoid contamination.

Dew and condensation can provide small but vital amounts of water. Early morning, dew collects on vegetation, tarps, and other surfaces. Using a clean cloth or directly wringing out vegetation can yield drinkable water. Additionally, placing a clean cloth or plastic sheet over vegetation in the evening can capture condensation, which can be wrung out in the morning.

A solar still extracts water from the soil and vegetation using the sun's heat. Water evaporates from the soil by digging a hole, placing a container in the center, and covering it with a transparent plastic sheet. It condenses on the plastic, eventually dripping into the container. This method can be used in various environments, including arid regions, to collect drinkable water.

Water can often be found in water heaters, toilet tanks (not the bowl), and pipes in urban environments. After shutting off the main water valve to prevent contaminated water from entering the system, water can be drained from these sources. Additionally, rainwater collection methods can be adapted to urban settings by using rooftops and gutters.

Regardless of the source, all water found in a grid-down situation should be considered potentially contaminated and purified before consumption, a process detailed in the following section. Practicing water conservation is also essential, prioritizing water usage for drinking and cooking over other activities.

Understanding how to locate water sources in various environments effectively can significantly increase your chances of survival in a grid-down scenario. Remember, the key to successful water procurement lies in knowing where to look and applying safe collection and purification methods to ensure the water is safe for consumption.

Methods of Water Purification

Once you have identified potential water sources, the next critical step is purifying the water to make it safe for consumption. Contaminated water can carry pathogens such as bacteria, viruses, and parasites, leading to severe illnesses. This section delves into various methods of water purification, each with its own set of advantages and considerations.

Boiling: Boiling is one of the most effective methods for purifying water. It kills most pathogens present in the water. To properly boil water, bring it to a rolling boil for at least one minute at sea level, adding one minute for every 1,000 feet of elevation above sea level. Although boiling does not remove chemical contaminants, it is effective against biological hazards.

Chemical Purification: Chemical purifiers, such as iodine or chlorine tablets, are convenient and lightweight options for treating water. Follow the manufacturer's instructions for the correct dosage and wait time. It's important to note that some pathogens, like Cryptosporidium, are resistant to chemical treatments. Additionally, these chemicals can leave an aftertaste, which can be mitigated by aerating the water or adding a pinch of salt.

UV Light Purification: Portable UV light purifiers are effective against bacteria, viruses, and protozoa. These devices work by exposing contaminated water to UV light, disrupting the DNA of pathogens and rendering them harmless. UV purification requires clear water so that pre-filtering may be necessary. It's also dependent on batteries or solar power, which could be a limitation in a grid-down scenario.

Filtration Systems: Water filters come in various forms, including pump filters, gravity filters, and straw filters. They physically remove pathogens and, depending on the pore size of the filter, can also eliminate chemicals and heavy metals. It's crucial to choose a filter that meets the EPA water purification standards and maintain it according to the manufacturer's guidelines.

Solar Disinfection (SODIS): This method involves filling clear plastic bottles with water and placing them in direct sunlight for at least six hours. The UV radiation from the sun kills pathogens. SODIS is a simple and cost-effective method, but it requires clear skies and relatively clear water. It's less effective in cloudy conditions or areas far from the equator.

Distillation: Distillation involves boiling water and then condensing the steam back into liquid. This process removes pathogens, heavy metals, salts, and contaminants. However, distillation requires a significant amount of fuel for boiling and a setup to condense the steam, making it less practical in some situations.

Each of these methods has its place in a comprehensive water purification strategy. The choice of method will depend on the specific circumstances, including the type and level of contamination, available resources, and the volume of water needed. In many cases, a combination of methods may be the most effective approach to ensure the safety of your water supply.

Storing and Conserving Water

Once you have procured and purified your water, the next critical step is to store and conserve it effectively. This ensures a sustainable supply, safeguarding against both contamination and scarcity. The strategies outlined here are designed to maximize your water reserves, ensuring they last as long as possible while remaining safe for consumption.

Choosing the Right Containers: The first step in storing water is selecting appropriate containers. Food-grade plastic containers with tight-fitting lids are ideal, as they are lightweight, durable, and do not impart harmful chemicals into the water. Glass containers are another safe option. However, they are heavier and more prone to breaking. Regardless of the material, ensure all containers are thoroughly cleaned and sanitized.

Location Matters: Store your water in a cool, dark place to prevent algae growth and keep the water from becoming too warm. Avoid direct sunlight and areas with significant temperature fluctuations. Basements or cellars can be ideal, but ensure containers are elevated off the ground on pallets or shelves to prevent contamination from flooding or spills.

Rotating Supplies: Water, while seemingly inert, can become stale or contaminated over time if not stored properly. To ensure freshness, label containers with the date of storage and rotate them regularly, using the oldest water first. This is especially important if you're using chlorine or other purification methods that diminish over time.

Mindful Usage: In a grid-down scenario, every drop counts. Be mindful of water usage, prioritizing drinking, cooking, and basic hygiene. Avoid wasting water on non-essential tasks. Simple habits, such as turning off the water while brushing your teeth or washing your hands with a minimal amount, can significantly extend your reserves.

Reusing Water: Consider ways to reuse water whenever safe and possible. For instance, water used for washing vegetables can be reused to water plants. Similarly, collecting rainwater can supplement your reserves, though it should be purified before drinking.

Leak Prevention: Regularly check your storage containers and any plumbing you may use for leaks. Even a small drip can result in significant water loss over time. Ensure all containers are tightly sealed and any hoses or faucets are turned off when not used.

Innovative Conservation Techniques: Explore innovative ways to conserve water, such as using water-saving devices or creating a rainwater collection system. Techniques like dew collection or solar stills can provide additional water sources in arid environments.

By implementing these storage and conservation strategies, you can ensure that your water supply remains robust and resilient, even in the most challenging grid-down scenarios. Water is life, and managing it wisely is paramount to survival.

Recognizing and Avoiding Contaminated Water

Ensuring the safety of your water supply is crucial to prevent severe illness and ensure survival. Water contamination can occur through biological, chemical, and physical pollutants, each posing unique risks. It's essential to understand the specific considerations for safe water consumption for each type of contaminant.

Biological contaminants include pathogens such as bacteria, viruses, and parasites, often found in water sources near populated areas or agricultural lands. Since signs of biological contamination are not always visible, it is best to treat any untreated water as potentially unsafe. Cloudy water, which has an unusual color or that contains organic material, should be treated with suspicion.

Chemical contaminants can enter water sources through industrial runoff, agricultural chemicals, and household waste. These contaminants may alter the taste, odor, or color of the water. Due to potential chemical pollution, it's advisable to avoid water from near industrial areas, mines, or agricultural fields.

Physical contaminants like sediments and metals can also pollute water. These are only sometimes harmful but can complicate water treatment. If water appears cloudy or has visible particles, it should be filtered before any disinfection process.

To avoid contaminated water, start by selecting water sources that are flowing and appear clear, ideally away from potential contamination sources. Always inspect the water visually for clarity, color, and floating materials. Although clear water is not a guarantee of safety, it is a preferable starting point for treatment.

Performing a smell test can also help avoid water with an unusual or strong odor, as it may be contaminated with chemicals or decaying organic matter. Tasting water to determine its safety is not recommended due to the risk of ingesting contaminants. If water tastes bad after treatment, it's safer to discard it and find an alternative source.

Always treat water from natural sources before consumption, regardless of its appearance or location. Boiling, filtration, and chemical disinfection are effective methods to make water safe. Be aware of your surroundings and potential upstream sources of contamination, as even remote streams can be affected by animal waste.

In urban environments, extra caution is needed with water from rivers, ponds, or lakes, which can accumulate pollutants from various sources. Understanding these risks and applying these guidelines can significantly reduce the risk of waterborne illness and ensure a safer water supply.

Rainwater Collection Techniques

Collecting rainwater is a sustainable method to achieve a reliable water source, providing relatively pure water and reducing dependence on potentially contaminated natural water bodies. The simplest form of rainwater collection involves using catchment areas such as roofs, followed by a conveyance system to direct the water into storage containers. It's crucial to ensure the catchment surface is made of non-toxic materials to avoid leaching harmful substances into the water. Metal roofs or those treated with non-toxic materials are ideal. The conveyance system, typically comprising gutters and downspouts, should be regularly cleaned to prevent blockages and contamination.

A first flush diverter is recommended to improve the quality of collected rainwater. This device diverts the initial flow of rainwater, which may contain contaminants from the catchment surface, away from the storage container. After the initial, most contaminated water is diverted, the cleaner water is allowed to flow into the storage system. This simple mechanism significantly enhances the purity of the collected water.

Food-grade barrels or tanks should be used to prevent chemicals from leaching into the water for storage. These containers must be covered to prevent mosquito breeding and debris entry. It's also advisable to place storage containers in a shaded area to inhibit algae growth. Non-scented household bleach (approximately 1/8 teaspoon per gallon) can be disinfectant for long-term storage. However, the treated water should stand for at least 30 minutes before use.

Even though rainwater is relatively clean, it can still be contaminated by airborne particles or materials from the catchment surface. Therefore, purification before consumption is essential. Boiling is the most effective method to kill pathogens. Alternatively, filtration systems can remove both particulates and microorganisms. Simple filters can be constructed using sand, charcoal, and gravel layers. For additional safety, chemical disinfectants like iodine or chlorine tablets can be used, following the manufacturer's instructions regarding dosage and contact time.

Regular maintenance of the rainwater collection system is crucial to ensure a safe water supply. This includes cleaning the catchment area, gutters, and storage containers. It's also essential to monitor the quality of the collected water, especially after prolonged dry spells or significant pollution events.

Implementing these rainwater collection techniques provides a sustainable solution to water procurement in a grid-down scenario. By understanding and applying these methods, individuals can secure a vital resource, ensuring their resilience and survival in challenging conditions.

Chapter Summary

- In a grid-down scenario, finding and purifying water is crucial for survival, with strategies varying by environment.
- Natural water sources like rivers and lakes can be used, but their quality must be assessed for contamination.
- Rainwater collection is a clean and simple method that uses containers or tarps to collect water.
- Dew and condensation offer small but vital water sources, which are collectible via clean cloths or plastic sheets.
- Solar stills can extract water from soil and vegetation using the sun's heat, making them suitable for arid regions.
- Urban environments offer water sources such as water heaters, toilet tanks, and rooftop rainwater collection.
- Water purification methods include boiling,

chemical treatment, UV light, filtration systems, solar disinfection (SODIS), and distillation.
- Proper storage and conservation of water through mindful usage, reusing, and preventing leaks are essential for maintaining a sustainable supply.

2
FOOD ACQUISITION AND STORAGE

Hunting and Trapping for Food

Hunting and trapping are vital skills for survival. These methods allow you to procure meat from the environment, a valuable source of protein and other nutrients essential for maintaining your strength and health.

Hunting involves pursuing wild animals for food. It requires knowledge of animal behavior, tracking skills, and the ability to effectively use weapons such as firearms or bows. Safety is paramount, not only in handling weapons but also in ensuring that you are hunting legally and ethically. Before a disaster strikes, please familiarize yourself with local wildlife species, their habits, and the best times for hunting them. Also, practice your shooting skills regularly and maintain your equipment to ensure reliability when it counts.

Trapping is another effective method for securing food. It can be more passive than hunting, allowing you to set up multiple traps that work for you while you attend to other survival tasks. Traps can be simple snares for small animals like rabbits and squirrels or more complex systems for larger game. Learning to set snares and traps requires practice, as improper setup can lead to failure in capturing the animal or, worse, injuring it without a humane outcome. It's also important to check your traps regularly to avoid suffering animals.

Both hunting and trapping demand a deep respect for nature and wildlife. They require patience, persistence, and a significant amount of knowledge. It's crucial to understand the laws that govern these activities in your area and to follow them strictly. In a survival situation, while you might need to rely more heavily on these skills, your responsibility is to manage resources sustainably. Overhunting or overtrapping can deplete local wildlife populations, making it even harder to find food in the future.

In addition to acquiring food through hunting and trapping, you must also know how to process and store the meat to ensure it lasts as long as possible without refrigeration. Techniques such as smoking, curing, and drying meat can preserve it for weeks or months. These methods provide a way to store food safely and add variety to your diet, which can be a welcome change in a prolonged survival scenario.

Remember, the key to effective hunting and trapping is

preparation. Invest time in learning and practicing these skills before they become a necessity. This preparation will boost your confidence and increase your chances of success in a grid-down world where self-sufficiency is the key to survival.

Foraging for Edible Plants

While hunting and trapping provide a valuable source of protein, foraging for edible plants is equally important as it supplements your diet with essential vitamins and minerals. Identifying edible plants accurately is crucial, as misidentification can lead to consuming toxic species, posing severe health risks. It's beneficial to start by familiarizing yourself with the flora in your region, focusing on easily recognizable and abundant species. Utilizing field guides specific to your area, which include color photographs and detailed descriptions, can be invaluable. Participating in local foraging workshops or hikes led by experienced foragers can enhance your skills.

Key plant identifiers include leaf shape, flower color and structure, fruit appearance, and growth patterns. It's important to cross-reference multiple identifiers to ensure accuracy, and while digital applications for plant identification can be helpful, they should be different from traditional knowledge and reference materials. When harvesting, it's vital to practice sustainability to ensure that plant populations remain healthy and viable for future use. This includes harvesting only what you need, using clean, sharp tools for precise cuts, and being mindful of the surrounding ecosystem.

Safety is paramount in foraging. You should never consume a plant unless you are 100% certain of its identification and are aware of potential allergic reactions. Avoid foraging near busy roads or industrial areas to prevent contamination from pollutants, and always wash all foraged foods thoroughly.

Focusing on a few common species like dandelion, wild garlic, wild onions, and blackberries can provide a solid foundation for your foraging efforts. These plants are widely found and easily identifiable and add flavor and nutritional benefits to meals. Once harvested, these edible plants can be incorporated into your diet in various ways. Leaves and greens can be used in salads or cooked, roots may be boiled or roasted, and berries and fruits can be eaten raw or used in jams and preserves.

In conclusion, foraging for edible plants is a valuable skill that enhances food security in a grid-down scenario. With the proper knowledge, identification skills, and safety precautions, the natural environment offers abundant nutritional resources. As we move forward, we will explore methods of preserving these and other foods without electricity, ensuring a varied and sustainable diet over the long term.

Preserving Food Without Electricity

Preserving food without the luxury of electricity becomes a paramount skill for survival. Traditional methods used for centuries help keep food safe and edible for extended periods, ensuring a stable food supply while maintaining nutritional value and taste. One of the oldest and most energy-efficient methods of food preservation is drying, which involves removing moisture from food to inhibit the growth of bacteria, yeast, and mold.

Fruits, vegetables, meats, and herbs can all be dried using sun drying, the simplest method suitable for hot, dry climates, or oven drying for those in less ideal climates. The key to successful drying is ensuring that all moisture is removed, which can be tested by the brittleness or leathery texture of the product. Smoking is another traditional method that preserves food and imparts a unique flavor, particularly suitable for meat and fish.

The smoking process involves hanging the food in a smoker or over a smoky fire for hours to days. This technique slowly cooks the food at low temperatures, helps dry it out, and adds an antimicrobial layer that protects against spoilage. Salting, or curing with salt, is another preservation method that draws moisture out of the food through osmosis, creating an environment inhospitable to microbial growth.

This method is especially effective for meats and fish, using either dry-curing with salt directly applied to the surface or wet-curing by soaking in a brine solution.

Fermentation relies on converting carbohydrates to alcohol or organic acids using microorganisms under anaerobic conditions, preserving the food, enhancing its nutritional value, and introducing probiotics into your diet. Common fermented foods include sauerkraut, kimchi, yogurt, and pickles, with successful fermentation depending on maintaining the correct temperature and salt concentration.

Root cellaring is a simple and effective way to store fruits and vegetables using the earth's natural insulation to maintain a consistent, cool, and humid environment. Vegetables like potatoes, carrots, beets, and fruits like apples and pears are well-suited for this method, with critical considerations including ventilation, temperature control, and humidity management. While traditional canning requires a heat source to process the jars, methods exist to preserve high-acid foods like fruits, tomatoes, and pickles without electricity using an open kettle and water bath canning over an open fire.

Incorporating these age-old preservation techniques into your survival strategy diversifies your food storage options and connects you to a heritage of self-sufficiency and resilience. Each method has advantages and challenges, and mastering them can significantly enhance your ability to sustain yourself and your loved ones in a grid-down scenario.

Creating a Survival Garden

A survival garden is essential for long-term food security in a grid-down scenario. It involves practical steps to create a garden that sustains and thrives, ensuring a steady food supply regardless of external circumstances. The first critical step is selecting an optimal site for your survival garden, which should receive at least six to eight hours of sunlight daily and have level ground to prevent water pooling. Container gardening or vertical gardening techniques can help maximize the growing area if space is limited.

Soil health is paramount in a survival garden. Start by testing the soil pH, aiming for a range between 6.0 and 7.0, and amend the soil with organic matter like compost to improve its structure, nutrient content, and water retention. Tilling the soil to a depth of at least 12 inches ensures that roots can penetrate deeply without obstruction.

Choosing suitable crops involves considering factors such as climate zone, growing season length, and the nutritional value of the plants. Focus on high-yield, nutrient-dense crops like potatoes, beans, squash, and leafy greens, and consider adding perennial crops like asparagus and berries for long-term yields. Heritage or heirloom varieties often provide better disease resistance and adaptability to local conditions.

Implement companion planting to maximize space, deter pests, and enhance growth, such as planting marigolds among tomatoes to repel harmful insects. Utilize succession planting by staggering planting dates or planting fast-growing crops between rows of longer-growing ones to ensure a continuous harvest. Efficient water management is crucial, especially in areas with limited water resources. Collect rainwater for irrigation and consider using drip irrigation or soaker hoses to minimize water waste.

Opt for organic methods for pest and disease control, introduce beneficial insects like ladybugs, and practice crop rotation to prevent soil-borne diseases. Regularly inspect plants and remove any signs of disease or infestation to prevent the spread. Harvest crops at their peak for the best nutritional value, save seeds from your best-performing plants to ensure a supply for the next planting season, and develop plant strains well-adapted to your garden conditions.

Creating a survival garden is a proactive step towards self-sufficiency, requiring planning, effort, and patience. The rewards include fresh, nutritious food and a deeper connection to the land, cultivating resilience and ensuring that you and your loved ones can thrive in the face of challenges.

Livestock and Animal Husbandry Basics

Understanding the role of livestock and animal husbandry is crucial for a sustainable food supply during grid-down scenarios. Transitioning from the cultivation of a survival garden, selecting the right livestock involves considering the size of your land, the climate, and your ability to provide for the animals. Chickens, rabbits, and goats are ideal for small-scale operations, providing eggs, meat, and dairy, while larger animals like cows and pigs might be feasible for those with more land.

Livestock requires appropriate shelter to protect it from the elements and predators, with the complexity varying by animal. For example, chickens need a coop, while goats and cows require sturdier structures like barns. Ensuring that animals have enough space to move and graze is also essential, as overcrowding can lead to disease and behavioral issues.

Feeding and nutrition are critical in a grid-down scenario where a self-sustaining approach is necessary. Animals like goats and cows can mainly graze but might need supplementary feed, including fodder crops from your garden, stored hay, or homemade feeds. Chickens and rabbits can benefit from kitchen scraps and garden waste, reducing the reliance on commercial feed.

Basic veterinary knowledge is essential for anyone raising livestock, including understanding common diseases and how to treat minor injuries. Establishing a relationship with a local veterinarian before a crisis is advisable, as is stockpiling essential veterinary supplies. Additionally, sustainable livestock management includes breeding and population control to ensure a continuous supply of animal products and maintain genetic diversity.

Integrating livestock with your survival garden can create a beneficial relationship where animals provide manure for compost and help control pests. However, it's essential to manage this integration to prevent crop damage. Livestock and animal husbandry are invaluable for a comprehensive food strategy in grid-down scenarios, requiring preparation, knowledge, and a commitment to animal well-being.

Chapter Summary

- Hunting and trapping are essential survival skills that provide a source of protein through the pursuit of wild animals and setting up traps for food.
- These activities require knowledge of animal behavior, legal and ethical considerations, and skills in weapon handling and trap setting, along with sustainable management of wildlife resources.
- Foraging for edible plants complements hunting and trapping by providing essential vitamins and minerals, emphasizing the importance of identifying and safely consuming wild edibles.
- Traditional food preservation methods without electricity, such as drying, smoking, salting, fermentation, and root cellaring, are vital for long-term food security.
- Establishing a survival garden with the right location, soil preparation, and crop selection ensures a steady food supply, focusing on high-yield, nutrient-dense crops.

- Efficient water management and organic pest control in gardening are essential, along with harvesting practices and seed saving for future planting.
- Livestock and animal husbandry, including selecting appropriate animals, providing shelter and nutrition, and managing health and breeding, complementing plant-based food sources.
- Integrating livestock with survival gardening creates a symbiotic relationship, enhancing soil fertility and pest control and contributing to a comprehensive food acquisition and storage strategy.

3
SHELTER AND SECURITY

Choosing a Safe Location

Finding and securing a safe location for shelter is essential. This decision can significantly impact your survival chances, affecting your immediate safety and your ability to gather resources, signal for help if necessary, and protect yourself from environmental hazards and potential threats.

When choosing a location for your shelter, the first factor to consider is the environmental conditions. Ideally, your shelter should be situated in an area that offers natural protection from the elements. Look for natural land formations such as hills or caves that shield you from strong winds, heavy rainfall, and extreme temperatures. However, be wary of locations that could become hazards themselves, such as flood plains or areas prone to landslides.

Accessibility to water is another critical factor. Your

shelter should be within a reasonable distance from a freshwater source. However, it's crucial to balance proximity with safety, as water sources can attract both animals and other survivors. Ensure your shelter is not directly visible from the water source to maintain stealth and security.

Visibility to others is a double-edged sword. While being wholly hidden can offer security, it may also hinder rescue efforts in scenarios where you seek to be found. Opt for a location that allows you to observe your surroundings without being easily spotted. Techniques such as camouflage or using natural vegetation for cover can be beneficial.

Consider the proximity to resources. Your shelter location should allow easy access to materials for building, firewood, and food sources. However, these resources should not be so close that they attract other people or wildlife directly to your shelter.

Lastly, consider the location's long-term viability. In a prolonged grid-down situation, you may need to stay in this shelter for an extended period. Assess the area for potential threats, including wildlife, environmental hazards, and human activity. A location that initially seems safe may become dangerous as conditions change or other survivors move into the area.

Choosing a safe location for your shelter is a critical decision that requires careful consideration of multiple factors. By prioritizing safety, accessibility to resources, and strategic visibility, you can significantly increase your chances of survival in a grid-down scenario. Once a suitable location has been identified, the next step is to build a temporary shelter that can protect you from the elements and provide a base for your survival efforts.

Building Temporary Shelters

This section delves into practical methods for building temporary shelters that can protect you from the elements and provide a degree of security in uncertain times. The focus here is on utilizing readily available materials and simple techniques that do not require advanced skills or tools.

The first approach to constructing a temporary shelter involves leveraging the natural resources around you. Look for natural formations such as caves, large rock overhangs, or dense foliage that can offer immediate protection without the need for significant alteration. If such natural shelters are not available, the environment often provides materials such as branches, leaves, and vines that can be used to construct a rudimentary shelter.

A simple lean-to shelter can be made by leaning branches against a fallen log or a sturdy, low-hanging branch of a living tree. The framework should then be covered with smaller branches, leaves, or any available foliage to create a windbreak and to insulate against the cold. Ensure the shelter is small enough to retain body heat but large enough to lie comfortably.

Consider improvised materials for shelter construction in urban environments or situations where natural materials are scarce. Tarps, blankets, and even large trash bags can be invaluable in creating a protective space. A tarp or a large piece of plastic can be tied between trees to form a simple tent-like structure that can shield you from rain and wind. Blankets can be used for additional warmth or as a ground cover to insulate from the cold earth.

Regardless of the materials used, insulation and waterproofing are vital considerations for any temporary shelter. In colder climates, insulation can be improved by piling leaves, grass, or even snow around and on top of your shelter. For waterproofing, ensure that the slope of any coverings allows rainwater to run off and not pool, potentially causing the shelter to collapse or become uninhabitable.

When constructing a temporary shelter, always consider your security. The shelter should be discreet, blending into the environment as much as possible to avoid drawing attention. It should also offer good visibility of the surrounding area, allowing you to see any approaching threats while remaining relatively concealed. Keep the shelter close to a water source but elevated to avoid flooding.

Building a temporary shelter in a grid-down scenario is about balancing the need for quick, adequate protection with the limitations of your environment and materials. Understanding and applying these basic principles can increase your chances of survival in the initial days following a disaster. Remember, the primary goal of any temporary shelter is to keep you safe and dry until you can either return home or transition to a more permanent habitat.

Constructing Long-Term Habitats

Transitioning from temporary shelters to constructing long-term habitats is the next logical step for survival. This section delves into the practicalities of building durable, secure, and sustainable living spaces that can support life for an extended period. The focus here is on selecting suitable locations, utilizing available materials, and incorporating renewable resources to create a stable environment.

Similarly to building a temporary habitat, the first step in constructing a long-term habitat is choosing an appropriate location. Factors to consider include proximity to water sources, elevation to avoid flooding, and natural barriers for protection against elements and potential threats. Assessing the land for agricultural potential is vital, ensuring that the soil can support crop cultivation for sustained food supply.

Utilizing locally available materials reduces the need for long-distance transportation and ensures that the habitat blends with the natural surroundings, offering camouflage against potential threats. Wood, stone, and earth are common materials that can be used effectively. Techniques such as timber framing, cob construction, and stone masonry are valuable skills to master, providing durable structures that can withstand harsh weather conditions.

In a grid-down situation, traditional utilities are no longer reliable. Renewable energy solutions such as solar panels or wind turbines can provide essential lighting, cooking, and heating power. Rainwater harvesting systems and gravity-fed water supplies can ensure a consistent water source, while water purification methods are crucial to ensure the water is safe for consumption.

Building with thermal mass in mind can help regulate indoor temperatures, keeping the habitat warm in the winter and cool in the summer. Materials like stone and earth absorb heat during the day and release it at night, reducing the need for external heating sources. Insulation is equally important, and natural materials such as straw bales or sheep's wool can be used effectively to prevent heat loss.

While the primary focus of a long-term habitat is sustainability and comfort, security should not be overlooked. Designing the habitat with a single, easily defendable entrance, incorporating hidden or disguised storage areas for supplies, and ensuring that windows are reinforced or situated to prevent easy access from the outside are all critical considerations.

Finally, constructing long-term habitats often requires a community effort. Sharing skills, labor, and resources can make the building process more efficient and foster a sense of community and mutual support, which is invaluable in a grid-down scenario. Establishing communication, trade, and defense agreements with nearby habitats can enhance security and resource availability.

Constructing a long-term habitat in a grid-down scenario

is complex but achievable. By carefully selecting a location, utilizing available materials, incorporating sustainable solutions, and focusing on security, survivors can create a stable and secure environment that supports long-term survival and well-being.

Home Fortification Techniques

Fortifying your long-term living space is crucial against potential threats. This section delves into practical home fortification techniques that can be implemented with minimal resources and technical know-how.

The first line of defense against intruders is to reinforce doors and windows. For doors, consider installing deadbolts and strike plates with longer screws to anchor them securely into the frame. A door barricade bar can also provide an additional layer of security. A simple but effective measure for sliding doors is to place a sturdy bar or a piece of wood in the track to prevent the door from being forced open.

Windows can be fortified by applying security film, which makes the glass more challenging to break. Installing window bars may also be necessary, especially in ground-level rooms. However, ensure that these measures do not trap occupants in case of a fire or other emergencies requiring quick evacuation.

To create a safe room, identify a room within your home that can be converted into a safe room. This room should have few or no windows and be accessible to all household members. Reinforce the door as you would the main entrance and stock the room with essential supplies, such as water, non-perishable food, a first aid kit, and a means of communication. This room can be a refuge during an extreme threat until help arrives or the situation stabilizes.

Improve visibility and deterrence. Good exterior lighting can deter would-be intruders. Solar-powered lights are ideal for grid-down situations, as they require no electricity. Position lights around the perimeter of your home, focusing on entry points and dark corners.

Consider also the strategic placement of security cameras. Even non-functional cameras can act as a deterrent. However, real-time monitoring capabilities can be advantageous if power solutions, such as solar panels or generators, are available.

Utilize natural and physical barriers. The landscape around your home can offer natural fortifications. Thorny bushes or dense hedges under windows can discourage attempts to break in. Similarly, a sturdy fence can serve as a physical barrier. While a high fence is beneficial, ensure that it does not provide cover for intruders to work unseen. The use of gravel in driveways and paths can alert you to visitors' approach due to the noise it generates when walked on.

Finally, in a grid-down scenario, there is strength in numbers. Collaborate with neighbors to establish a neighborhood watch or mutual aid agreements. Sharing information and resources can significantly enhance the security of your home and the community.

By implementing these home fortification techniques, you can create a safer and more secure environment for you and your family in the face of uncertainty. The next step in ensuring your safety involves developing comprehensive security measures and perimeter defense strategies to protect your fortified home further.

Security Measures and Perimeter Defense

With the basic fortification of your home addressed, the focus must now shift towards establishing a robust perimeter defense. This involves a combination of physical barriers, surveillance, and strategic planning to deter potential threats and ensure the safety of inhabitants.

Physical Barriers: The first line of defense in perimeter security is the creation of physical barriers. These can range from simple obstacles like fences and walls to more sophisticated ones like trenches or natural barriers like thick hedges. The key is to create a barrier that is difficult to cross unnoticed. Fences should be tall enough to deter climbers and include features like barbed wire to discourage attempts to breach them. On the other hand, walls offer more durability and can be reinforced with materials that make them difficult to penetrate.

Surveillance: In a grid-down situation, traditional electronic surveillance systems may not be reliable. However, alternative methods of surveillance can be employed. Setting up observation posts at strategic points around the perimeter allows for continuously monitoring the surroundings. These posts should be well-camouflaged and manned by individuals trained in spotting and assessing potential threats. Additionally, using mirrors or reflective surfaces can help extend the field of view around corners or over obstacles.

Alarm Systems: While electronic alarms may be inoperative, improvised alarm systems can be valuable to your security measures. Simple tripwires connected to noisy objects can be an early warning system against intruders. Cans filled with pebbles or bells attached to strings can create enough noise to alert defenders without requiring any power source.

Natural Surveillance: Utilizing the natural landscape can significantly enhance perimeter defense. Clearing foliage and potential hiding spots near your shelter eliminates cover for would-be intruders. Conversely, planting thorny bushes or other natural barriers can provide an eco-friendly deterrent that requires minimal maintenance.

Access Control: Controlling access to your shelter is crucial. This means establishing secure entry and exit points that can be easily monitored and defended. Gates should be sturdy and lockable, with reinforced hinges and locks that are difficult to tamper with. Ideally, the shelter should have a single, well-defended entrance, with all other potential access points securely sealed.

Community Coordination: In situations where multiple shelters are nearby, coordinating with neighboring shelters can create a mutual defense network. Sharing surveillance duties and establishing standard alarm signals can enhance the security of all involved. This collective approach distributes the workload and creates a more robust defense against external threats.

Training and Drills: Finally, the effectiveness of any security measure is only as good as the people implementing it. Regular training sessions and drills should be conducted to ensure that all inhabitants are familiar with security protocols, surveillance techniques, and emergency response procedures. This preparation ensures that in the event of an actual threat, everyone knows their role and can act swiftly and efficiently to secure the shelter.

By implementing these security measures and perimeter defense strategies, you can significantly enhance the safety and security of your shelter in a grid-down scenario. Remember, the goal is to deter potential threats and provide peace of mind for the inhabitants, knowing that measures are in place to protect them in uncertain times.

Fire Safety and Management

Fire is great. It's a crucial tool for warmth, cooking, and signaling. But, fire can become a devastating force if not properly managed. Especially when conventional emergency services are unavailable. This section delves into the essential fire safety and management practices to ensure your shelter remains a safe haven during challenging times.

First and foremost, selecting the appropriate location for your fire is critical. When outdoors, choose a spot that is clear of overhead hazards, such as tree branches, and at least 15 feet away from tent walls, shrubbery, and other flammable materials. Creating a perimeter of rocks or digging a small pit can help contain the fire and prevent it from spreading. For indoor fires, such as those in a fireplace or wood stove, ensure that the structure is well-ventilated to avoid smoke and carbon monoxide buildup. Regular inspection and cleaning of chimneys and flues are imperative to prevent blockages and reduce the risk of chimney fires.

Equally important is the selection of fuel for your fire. Dry, seasoned wood burns more efficiently and produces less smoke than green or wet wood. In a grid-down situation, conserving resources is critical, so use your fuel judiciously. Start with smaller kindling to get the fire going before adding larger logs to maintain it. This method reduces waste and minimizes the risk of creating an uncontrollably large fire.

Fire extinguishing practices are another critical component of fire safety. Always have a plan for extinguishing your fire quickly and safely. Keeping a bucket of water, sand, or dirt nearby for outdoor fires can allow for rapid response if the fire spreads. In an indoor setting, ensure you have a functional fire extinguisher within reach and that all occupants are familiar with its operation. Before leaving a fire unattended, whether indoors or out, ensure it is completely extinguished. Coals can remain hot and reignite for hours or even days after the flames have died.

Lastly, fire safety education is an invaluable tool. Familiarize yourself and your group with basic fire safety practices, such as "stop, drop, and roll," and establishing clear escape routes during a fire. Regular drills and discussions about fire safety help ensure everyone knows how to act swiftly and safely should a fire emergency arise.

In conclusion, while fire is an indispensable survival tool, its potential for destruction necessitates a disciplined approach to safety and management. By selecting appropriate fire locations, using fuel efficiently, practicing safe extinguishing methods, and prioritizing fire safety education, you can significantly reduce the risks associated with fire in a grid-down scenario, ensuring your shelter remains a secure and safe environment for all occupants.

Chapter Summary

- Choosing a safe location for shelter is crucial for survival in a grid-down scenario.
- Use natural resources and improvised materials to build shelters that protect from the elements.
- Transition to long-term habitats by selecting suitable locations and using local materials.
- Reinforce doors and windows to secure your home against threats.
- Establish a robust perimeter defense to ensure the safety of inhabitants.

- Practice fire safety by choosing appropriate locations and having extinguishing plans.
- Strategic location selection and resource accessibility are essential for survival and security.
- Emphasize community effort in constructing long-term habitats and fortifying homes.

4
HEALTH AND FIRST AID

Basic First Aid Skills

In grid-down survival, a foundational understanding of basic first aid skills is not just beneficial but crucial. The ability to respond effectively to common injuries and illnesses can mean the difference between a minor inconvenience and a life-threatening situation. This section aims to equip you with the knowledge and confidence needed to handle such scenarios, ensuring you're prepared for various medical emergencies that might arise when professional medical help is not immediately accessible.

First and foremost, it's essential to understand the principles of assessing a situation before diving into action. Always ensure the scene is safe for both the responder (you) and the victim. This means checking for any ongoing dangers, such as fire, toxic gas, or unstable structures. Once it's safe to proceed, assess the victim's condition by checking their responsiveness, airway, breathing, and circulation—often called the ABCs of first aid.

For unresponsive individuals, immediate action may be required. CPR (Cardiopulmonary Resuscitation) may be necessary if they are not breathing. It's crucial to be trained in performing CPR correctly, as improper technique can do more harm than good. Remember, CPR for adults differs from that for children and infants, so specialized training for each category is advisable.

Bleeding is another common issue that can arise in various situations, from minor cuts to severe wounds. The primary goal is to control the bleeding. Apply direct pressure to the wound with a clean cloth or bandage. If the bleeding does not stop, elevate the wound above the heart level and continue applying pressure. It's important to keep the person calm and still, as movement can exacerbate bleeding.

Burns, ranging from minor to severe, require specific care. For minor burns, cool the area under running water for at least 10 minutes to reduce pain and swelling. Avoid using ice, as it can cause further damage to the skin. Cover the burn with a sterile, non-adhesive bandage or cloth. For more severe burns, do not apply water. Instead, cover the burn with a clean, dry cloth and seek medical attention immediately.

Immobilization is key in cases of fractures or sprains. Use splints made from available materials to stabilize the affected area and prevent further injury. Ensure the splint is not too tight, as this can impede circulation. The RICE method (Rest,

Ice, Compression, Elevation) can effectively reduce swelling and pain for sprains.

Recognizing the signs of common illnesses is also vital. Symptoms such as fever, vomiting, diarrhea, or rash may indicate various conditions that require different approaches. Hydration is crucial, especially in cases of vomiting and diarrhea. Monitor the person's temperature and provide over-the-counter medications if appropriate and available.

Lastly, always remember the importance of personal protection. Utilize gloves if available when dealing with blood or bodily fluids to minimize the risk of infection. Wash your hands thoroughly before and after providing first aid.

By mastering these basic first aid skills, you'll be better prepared to handle common injuries and illnesses, providing crucial care in the critical moments that often precede professional medical treatment. This knowledge enhances your survival capabilities and empowers you to assist others in need, embodying the essence of preparedness and resilience in grid-down scenarios.

Handling Common Injuries and Illnesses

Without access to professional medical facilities, primary healthcare responsibility falls squarely on the shoulders of individuals and communities. This section delves into practical strategies for managing various health concerns likely to arise, emphasizing a hands-on approach to care.

Cuts, from minor to severe, are among the most common

injuries. Immediate and proper care is essential to prevent infection and ensure healing. Begin by washing your hands to minimize the risk of introducing bacteria into the wound. If available, wear gloves for additional protection. Clean the wound gently with water and mild soap, avoiding the use of harsh chemicals that can irritate the injury. Apply direct pressure with a clean cloth to stop bleeding. Once bleeding has ceased, cover the wound with a sterile bandage. Change the dressing daily or whenever it becomes wet or dirty. Watch for signs of infection, such as redness, swelling, or pus, and take steps to address these symptoms promptly.

Sprains and strains frequently occur during physical activity, especially in uneven or unfamiliar terrain. A sprain affects ligaments, the fibrous tissue connecting bones, while a strain involves muscles or tendons. The RICE method (Rest, Ice, Compression, Elevation) is a time-tested approach to treatment. Rest the injured area, apply ice to reduce swelling (wrapped in a cloth to avoid skin damage), use a compression bandage to provide support, and elevate the injury above heart level when possible. Limit movement until healing has progressed, and gradually reintroduce activity to avoid stiffness and encourage strength rebuilding.

Burns, whether from fire, sun exposure, or contact with hot objects, require careful attention. For minor burns, cool the area under running water for several minutes to reduce pain and swelling. Do not apply ice directly, as this can cause further damage to the skin. Cover the burn with a sterile, non-adhesive bandage or cloth. Avoid ointments or butter, which can trap heat and worsen the injury. For more severe burns characterized by extensive damage or charring of the skin, seek professional medical help immediately.

Dehydration and heat exhaustion are serious risks, particularly in hot climates or during strenuous activity. Symptoms include thirst, dizziness, fatigue, and confusion. Prevent dehydration by drinking plenty of water, even before feeling thirsty. For someone experiencing heat exhaustion, move them to a cooler place, encourage them to drink water or electrolyte solutions, and cool their body with wet cloths or a bath. Rest is crucial until recovery is evident.

In situations where sanitation is compromised, gastrointestinal issues can become common. Preventative measures include practicing good hygiene and ensuring water and food safety. For mild cases of diarrhea, maintain hydration with small, frequent sips of water or oral rehydration solutions. Avoid solid foods until symptoms improve. If symptoms persist or are severe, especially in children or the elderly, seek ways to access professional medical advice.

The ability to adapt and apply basic healthcare principles is invaluable in a grid-down scenario. While this guide covers managing common injuries and illnesses, it's important to continue learning and practicing these skills. Knowledge, preparation, and calm can significantly impact health outcomes in challenging situations.

Natural Remedies and Alternative Medicines

When conventional medical treatments are inaccessible, natural remedies and alternative medicines become essential. These traditional healing practices and plant-based treatments have been used for centuries. Practical, accessible, and effective natural remedies that can be cultivated or foraged provide a crucial lifeline when modern healthcare is unavailable.

Herbs are pivotal in traditional medicine across cultures, treating everything from minor headaches and digestive issues to inflammation and infections. Due to its salicin content, Willow bark, which is often called nature's aspirin, helps alleviate pain, reduce fever, and ease inflammation. Lavender is valued for its calming effects and antiseptic properties, and it is helpful for stress relief and treating cuts. Peppermint effectively addresses digestive problems and headaches. Echinacea is commonly used to bolster the immune system and combat respiratory infections.

In addition to cultivated herbs, many wild plants like dandelion, plantain, and yarrow offer medicinal benefits. Dandelions are nutritious and support liver health, plantain leaves soothe skin irritations and cuts, and yarrow is essential for first aid, capable of stopping bleeding and reducing fever. The effectiveness of these natural remedies largely depends on their proper preparation and usage. Infusions and decoctions extract medicinal properties from plants, while tinctures provide a potent, preserved form of herbal remedies.

However, using natural remedies requires caution. Accurate plant identification is critical to avoid harmful mistakes, and proper dosages ensure safety. Awareness of potential allergies and interactions with other medications is also necessary. In conclusion, natural remedies and alternative medicines are valuable for maintaining health and treating ailments when conventional options fail. By learning about herbal and plant medicine, individuals can enhance their resilience and self-sufficiency, preparing to care for themselves and their loved ones in challenging times.

Maintaining Hygiene and Sanitation

Maintaining hygiene and sanitation when the grid is down is crucial to prevent disease. Personal hygiene is essential; wash your hands regularly with soap and water, especially before eating, after using the toilet, and when handling food. If water is scarce, use alcohol-based hand sanitizers or a homemade solution of 1 part bleach to 9 parts water.

Try to bathe regularly using minimal water; sponge baths can be an effective way to conserve water while still cleaning the skin. If functioning toilets are unavailable, create a restroom away from living areas and water sources. Dig a deep hole for waste and cover it with soil after each use to reduce odor and deter flies, or use a bucket lined with a plastic bag indoors, sealing and disposing of it properly.

Proper disposal is critical; separate organic waste from recyclables and non-biodegradable materials. Compost organic waste reduces volume and creates beneficial soil while storing non-biodegradable waste securely until proper disposal is possible. Avoid burning waste due to pollution and fire risks.

Safe drinking water is necessary; boil water for at least one minute to kill pathogens or use purification tablets or household bleach if boiling isn't possible. Store purified water in clean, covered containers. Food safety is also essential; cover food to protect it from pests, cook thoroughly, and rely on non-perishable items like canned goods and dried foods. Wash fruits and vegetables with purified water before consumption.

Control pests by keeping living areas clean, sealing gaps, and using traps or natural repellents. Mosquito nets can offer protection during sleep. Be vigilant for signs of illness and isolate sick individuals early to prevent spread. Use natural remedies and over-the-counter medications for minor issues, and seek medical help for severe conditions when possible. Following these guidelines can significantly reduce disease risk and create a safer environment.

Preventing and Treating Waterborne Diseases

Waterborne diseases such as cholera, dysentery, and typhoid pose significant health risks, notably lacking sanitation and hygiene. Practical strategies for preventing and treating these diseases include water purification, recognizing symptoms, and understanding basic treatment methods. Ensuring that drinking water is free from pathogens is crucial for prevention. Boiling water is a highly effective method; it should be brought to a rolling boil for at least one or three minutes at higher altitudes to kill most pathogens. Alternatively, chemical disinfectants like chlorine dioxide or iodine tablets can be used, though they may not eliminate all pathogens and could alter the water's taste.

For a sustainable approach, consider installing a rainwater collection system or using a high-quality water filter to remove contaminants. Clear water isn't necessarily safe for consumption and must be treated. Early recognition of waterborne disease symptoms such as diarrhea, vomiting, fever, and abdominal cramps is vital for effective treatment. Dehydration is a significant concern, indicated by symptoms like thirst, reduced urination, dry skin, fatigue, and dizziness. Recognizing these signs early can facilitate quicker treatment and recovery.

The primary treatment for waterborne diseases involves rehydration. For mild dehydration, consuming clean, purified water is crucial. In more severe cases, oral rehydration solutions (ORS) are essential and can be life-saving. ORS packets are practical for medical kits, but a homemade solution can also be made from salt, sugar, and treated water. Medical intervention with antibiotics or other medications may be necessary for persistent or severe symptoms, but these should be administered under professional guidance to avoid complications such as antibiotic resistance. In summary, managing waterborne diseases effectively requires proper water treatment, prompt recognition of symptoms, and immediate rehydration. These measures are crucial to maintaining health and resilience in challenging conditions.

Mental Health and Coping Mechanisms

An often overlooked aspect of survival is mental health and well-being. The psychological impact of such events can be profound, affecting individuals' ability to make rational decisions, maintain relationships, and ultimately survive. This section delves into the significance of mental health and coping mechanisms that can be employed to navigate through the psychological challenges of a grid-down situation.

Mental health challenges in a grid-down scenario can range from acute stress reactions to more prolonged disorders such as depression and post-traumatic stress disorder (PTSD). The loss of normalcy, the uncertainty of the future, and the potential for significant lifestyle changes or losses can trigger these responses. Recognizing the signs of mental health distress in oneself and others becomes a critical skill. Symptoms may include persistent sadness, excessive worry, changes in sleep patterns, withdrawal from social interactions, and increased irritability or aggression.

Establishing a routine can provide a sense of normalcy and control to mitigate these challenges. Even in chaos, a structured daily schedule that includes time for physical activity, rest, meals, and social interaction can help maintain mental balance. Physical exercise, in particular, is beneficial not only for physical health but also for mental well-being, as it can reduce symptoms of anxiety and depression.

Social support plays a pivotal role in coping with stress and trauma. Building and maintaining a trust network with fellow survivors can provide emotional comfort and practical assistance. Sharing experiences and feelings with others who understand the situation can alleviate isolation and help process emotions.

Practicing mindfulness and relaxation techniques can also effectively manage stress and anxiety. Techniques such as deep breathing, meditation, and progressive muscle relaxation can help calm the mind and reduce the physiological responses to stress. These practices can be particularly beneficial in situations where the environment is beyond one's control, helping individuals focus on the present moment and reduce anxiety about the future.

In addition to these self-help strategies, it's important to recognize when professional help is needed. In a grid-down scenario, access to mental health professionals may be limited, but utilizing any available resources, such as counselors or support hotlines, can be crucial for those experiencing severe mental health difficulties.

Lastly, engaging in purposeful activities that contribute to the community's well-being can enhance one's sense of purpose and belonging. Whether participating in rebuilding efforts, teaching valuable skills to others, or simply offering a listening ear, being part of something larger than oneself can provide a powerful counterbalance to the feelings of despair and helplessness that may arise.

In conclusion, while the challenges of surviving a grid-down scenario are manifold, the importance of mental health cannot be overstated. Individuals can bolster their psychological resilience by employing a range of coping mechanisms, from maintaining routines and exercising to seeking social support and engaging in community activities. This, in turn, enhances their overall capacity to navigate the complexities of a post-grid-down world, ensuring survival and a path toward recovery and rebuilding.

Chapter Summary

- Understanding basic first aid skills is crucial for survival in grid-down scenarios. These skills enable individuals to handle medical emergencies when professional help is unavailable.
- Key first aid principles include scene safety and the ABCs (Airway, Breathing, Circulation); CPR may be necessary for unresponsive individuals, with different techniques for adults, children, and infants.
- Controlling bleeding involves applying direct pressure, elevating the wound, and keeping the injured person calm. Depending on the severity of the burn, it requires cooling with water or covering with a clean cloth.

- Fractures and sprains need immobilization and possibly the RICE method (Rest, Ice, Compression, Elevation); recognizing common illness signs and ensuring hydration is vital.
- Personal protection, like using gloves and washing hands, is important when providing first aid to minimize infection risk.
- Handling common injuries like cuts, sprains, burns, and addressing dehydration, gastrointestinal issues, and ensuring hygiene and sanitation are emphasized for health maintenance in grid-down situations.
- Natural and alternative medicines, including herbal and medicinal plants, offer viable treatment options when conventional healthcare is unavailable. They also have safety considerations for identification, dosages, and allergies.
- Mental health is as crucial as physical health, with coping mechanisms such as establishing routines, exercising, seeking social support, practicing mindfulness, and engaging in community activities highlighted for psychological resilience.

5

ENERGY AND POWER ALTERNATIVES

Solar Power Basics

Solar power is great, particularly in scenarios where traditional power grids are no longer reliable. This section delves into the fundamentals of harnessing solar energy, which converts the sun's rays into usable electricity, offering a lifeline in times of energy scarcity.

At the heart of solar power systems are solar panels composed of photovoltaic (PV) cells. These cells are designed to capture sunlight and convert it into direct current (DC) electricity. The efficiency of this conversion process is a critical factor, influenced by the quality of the solar panels, the angle at which they are installed, and the amount of sunlight they receive. For optimal performance, panels should be positioned to face true south (in the Northern Hemisphere) and tilted at an angle equal to the latitude of their location, though adjustments may be necessary to account for seasonal variations in the sun's path.

Once generated, the DC electricity must still be prepared for typical household use. Most homes and appliances operate on alternating current (AC), necessitating an inverter. This device converts DC into AC, making the electricity compatible with the grid and suitable for everyday consumption. Modern inverters also have monitoring capabilities, allowing users to track their system's performance and energy output in real time.

For those living off-grid or in areas prone to power outages, energy storage is a crucial component of a solar power system. Batteries enable the storage of excess electricity produced during peak sunlight hours for use at night or on cloudy days. Lead-acid and lithium-ion batteries are the most common types, each with advantages and considerations regarding capacity, lifespan, and maintenance.

Implementing a solar power system requires careful planning and consideration of several factors, including location, energy needs, and budget. Initial costs can be significant, but various incentives and rebates governments and utilities offer can help offset these expenses. Moreover, the long-term benefits—reduced reliance on the grid, lower electricity bills, and a smaller carbon footprint—make solar power an increasingly attractive option for those seeking energy independence.

In embracing solar power, individuals secure a reliable energy source for themselves and contribute to a larger movement towards sustainable living. As we transition to the next section, we'll explore another form of renewable energy that complements solar power, offering further resilience and self-sufficiency in a grid-down scenario.

Wind Energy Fundamentals

Wind energy is a sustainable and reliable energy source in a grid-down scenario. This section delves into the fundamentals of harnessing wind power, a resource that has been utilized for centuries but remains underexploited in modern survival strategies.

Wind energy is generated by converting kinetic energy from wind into mechanical power or electricity. This process is facilitated by wind turbines, which consist of blades mounted on a tower to capture wind energy. When the wind blows, it turns the turbine's blades around a rotor, which spins a generator to produce electricity.

The feasibility of wind power as a survival energy source hinges on several factors, including location, wind speed, and the availability of suitable technology. Wind speeds vary greatly depending on geographic location, terrain, and altitude. Generally, an area with average wind speeds of at least 10 miles per hour (mph) is suitable for small-scale wind power generation. It's crucial to thoroughly assess local wind resources to determine the viability of wind energy in a specific location.

Small wind turbines can be a practical option for those in

areas conducive to wind power. These turbines can be installed on properties to generate electricity for individual homes or small communities. A wind turbine's capacity is measured in kilowatts (kW), with systems typically ranging from 1 kW to 10 kW for residential use. The amount of electricity a turbine can generate depends on its capacity, the wind speed, and the turbine's efficiency.

When considering the installation of a wind turbine, the initial costs, which include the turbine, tower, inverter, and installation, must be taken into account. Despite these upfront expenses, wind energy can be a cost-effective solution over time, particularly in off-grid scenarios where traditional power sources are unavailable or unsustainable.

Maintenance is another critical aspect of wind power. Regular inspections and upkeep are necessary to ensure the longevity and efficiency of the system. This includes checking the turbine's components for wear and tear, ensuring the blades are free of obstructions, and verifying that electrical connections are secure.

Incorporating wind energy into a grid-down survival plan offers several advantages. It provides a renewable and clean source of electricity, reduces dependence on fossil fuels, and can be combined with other renewable energy sources, such as solar power, to create a more robust and reliable energy system.

As we transition from discussing the potential of solar energy, it's clear that wind power represents another vital component in the arsenal of renewable energy options for sustainable living in times of crisis. By understanding the fundamentals of wind energy, individuals and communities can better prepare for and adapt to the challenges of a grid-down scenario, ensuring access to essential power when it's most needed.

Hydro Power Options

Hydropower is a viable and often underutilized energy source in sustainable and off-grid living. It involves converting the energy from flowing or falling water into electricity, using a simple principle: water turns a turbine, which spins a generator to produce electricity. The implementation of this principle varies based on available water sources, geographic conditions, and specific energy needs.

One accessible form of hydropower for off-grid living is the micro-hydro system, which generates power from small streams or rivers. These systems consist of an intake where water is diverted, a penstock (pipe) leading the water to the turbine, the turbine itself, a generator, and a tailrace where water returns to the stream. Micro-hydro provides continuous, reliable power and requires relatively low maintenance, making it ideal for those near suitable water sources.

Selecting the right site for a hydropower installation is crucial. To maximize power output, a sufficient water flow must be combined with a significant drop in elevation. Environmental and regulatory factors must also be considered, as water diversion and construction may impact ecosystems and require permits. For DIY enthusiasts, building a hydropower system can be rewarding, using off-the-shelf components and online tutorials for guidance. Safety measures such as proper grounding and waterproofing are essential.

Integrating hydropower into an off-grid system often involves using a battery bank for electricity storage, allowing the system to provide power during low water flow and meet varying demands. Components like charge controllers and inverters manage and convert the electricity for household use. In conclusion, hydropower is a promising alternative for those seeking grid independence or supplementing their energy sources sustainably, playing a pivotal role in off-grid living and emergency preparedness.

Manual Power Generation Techniques

This section delves into the practical and innovative techniques of manual power generation, offering a lifeline in scenarios where conventional energy sources are unavailable or have been compromised.

Hand Crank Generators: These devices convert human mechanical energy into electrical energy by turning a crank. Hand crank generators are invaluable for charging small devices such as radios, flashlights, and mobile phones. Their efficiency, however, is directly proportional to the physical effort exerted, making them more suitable for low-power applications or as a temporary solution during energy shortages.

Bicycle Generators: A step up from hand crank generators, bicycle generators harness the power of pedaling to produce electricity. By attaching a stationary bike to a generator, individuals can produce more power and be capable of charging larger batteries or running small appliances. The setup usually involves a motor used as a generator, a belt drive, and a charge controller to regulate the energy produced. This method not only provides a sustainable source of power but also promotes physical fitness.

Manual Treadmill Generators: Similar in concept to the bicycle generator, manual treadmill generators convert kinetic energy from walking or running into electrical power. Though the initial setup might require some technical adjustments, the energy output can be significant, making it a viable option for powering essential devices in a grid-down scenario.

Hand-Powered Flashlights and Radios: These devices have built-in generators activated by squeezing a handle or winding a crank. They are particularly useful in emergency kits, providing light and access to information without the need for external power sources. Their ease of use and portability make them indispensable tools for survival situations.

DIY Wind Turbines: For those with a knack for engineering and access to basic materials, constructing a DIY wind turbine can effectively generate power manually. Individuals can create a wind power system capable of charging batteries and powering small appliances using salvaged parts such as motorbike alternators, PVC pipes for blades, and repurposed batteries for storage. While this requires a higher level of technical skill, the payoff for renewable energy production can be substantial.

Incorporating these manual power generation techniques into your survival strategy ensures a degree of independence from the grid and prepares you for a wide range of emergency scenarios. Each method offers unique advantages and challenges, allowing for customization based on individual needs, physical capabilities, and available resources. As we move forward, the next logical step in ensuring a comprehensive energy solution in grid-down situations is to explore practical battery storage and management strategies, ensuring that the power generated through these manual methods is stored efficiently and ready for use when needed.

Battery Storage and Management

Storing and managing power efficiently is as crucial as generating it, especially when traditional power sources are unavailable. Understanding the different types of batteries available is the first step in mastering battery storage. The most common types include lead-acid, lithium-ion, nickel-cadmium (NiCd), and nickel-metal hydride (NiMH).

Lead-acid batteries are the oldest type of rechargeable battery. They are widely used due to their cost-effectiveness and high surge capability. However, they are heavy and have a lower energy density. Lithium-ion batteries are known for their high energy density and lightweight, making them prevalent in modern electronics and electric vehicles. They charge faster and have a longer lifespan than lead-acid batteries but are more expensive.

Nickel-cadmium batteries can deliver full power until completely discharged and withstand extreme temperatures and rough handling. However, they suffer from the "memory effect" and contain toxic materials. Nickel-metal hydride batteries offer a higher energy density than NiCd without toxic components. They are less prone to the memory effect but have a shorter lifespan in high-drain devices.

Proper storage extends the life of batteries and ensures they are ready when needed. Storing batteries in a cool, dry place helps maintain performance, as extreme temperatures can degrade them. Lithium-ion batteries should be kept at a 40-50% charge state for long-term storage, while lead-acid batteries should be fully charged and topped off every three to six months.

A Battery Management System (BMS) is crucial for monitoring and managing the health and performance of a battery pack. It performs cell balancing, overcharge and over-discharge protection, and temperature monitoring. These functions help prolong the battery's lifespan and prevent damage.

A battery bank is an effective strategy for maintaining a substantial power reserve. This involves connecting multiple batteries in series or parallel to increase voltage or amp-hour capacity. It is essential to use batteries of the same type, age, and capacity to prevent imbalance and to use proper cabling and connectors to ensure efficient power flow.

In conclusion, understanding and implementing adequate battery storage and management practices are pivotal in ensuring a reliable energy supply in grid-down scenarios. One can significantly enhance their energy resilience by selecting the appropriate battery types, adhering to storage best practices, utilizing a BMS, and carefully designing a battery bank. Integrating these storage solutions into a broader renewable energy plan is the next step toward achieving sustainable, off-grid power independence.

Creating a Renewable Energy Plan

Creating a renewable energy plan is a matter of convenience and survival. This section delves into the practical steps and considerations in establishing a renewable energy system that can sustain your needs during extended periods without grid power.

First and foremost, it's essential to assess your energy needs accurately. Begin by listing all the essential devices and appliances, such as refrigeration for food preservation, lighting, heating or cooling systems, and communication devices. For each item, note its power consumption in watts and estimate how many hours per day it will be used. This exercise will give you a rough estimate of your daily energy requirements in watt-hours (Wh) or kilowatt-hours (kWh), which is crucial for designing an appropriately sized renewable energy system.

Once you have a clear understanding of your energy needs, the next step is to explore the feasible renewable energy options for your location. Solar power is the most accessible and widely applicable option, but wind, hydro, and pedal power could be viable depending on your circumstances. Each energy source has advantages and limitations, which must be carefully considered. For instance, solar panels require significant sunlight exposure, making them less effective in areas with prolonged periods of cloud cover or during the winter months in higher latitudes.

The choice of renewable energy sources will directly influence the equipment you need. For solar power, this includes photovoltaic (PV) panels, inverters to convert the DC electricity generated by the panels into AC electricity usable by household devices, and mounting hardware. Wind power systems require turbines, towers, and, again, inverters. If you're considering multiple energy sources, you'll also need a controller to manage the input from each source efficiently.

Integration with your battery storage system is the next critical step. The energy generated by your renewable sources must be stored effectively when the source isn't actively generating power (e.g., solar panels at night). This involves selecting batteries with sufficient capacity to meet your energy needs and configuring them for optimal charge and discharge cycles. The connection between your renewable energy generation and battery storage must be carefully managed to prevent overcharging or excessive depletion, which can significantly reduce the lifespan of your batteries.

Maintenance and monitoring are ongoing requirements for a renewable energy system. Regular checks will ensure that your equipment is functioning correctly and efficiently. This includes cleaning solar panels or wind turbine blades to remove dust and debris, checking connections for corrosion or wear, and monitoring system output to identify any issues promptly.

Finally, it's important to consider redundancy and backup options. No system is fail-proof, and having alternative means of meeting your essential energy needs can provide peace of mind and additional security in a grid-down scenario. This could be as simple as having portable solar chargers for small devices, manual tools to replace electric ones, or even a backup generator for critical needs, though the latter relies on fuel that may also be in short supply.

Creating a renewable energy plan is a significant undertaking that requires careful planning, investment, and ongoing management. However, its independence and security in a grid-down situation make it an essential component of any comprehensive survival strategy. By assessing your needs, choosing the right mix of renewable sources, and ensuring proper integration and maintenance, you can establish a resilient energy system that sustains your essential needs when the grid is down.

Chapter Summary

- Solar power basics highlight the importance of solar panels and photovoltaic (PV) cells in converting sunlight into electricity, emphasizing the need for optimal panel positioning and inverters to convert DC to AC electricity for household use.
- Energy storage, particularly through batteries like lead-acid and lithium-ion, is crucial for off-grid solar systems to provide electricity during the night or cloudy days, with incentives and rebates available to offset initial costs.
- Wind energy is presented as a sustainable alternative, with wind turbines converting kinetic energy from wind into electricity, dependent on factors like location, wind speed, and technology for feasibility.
- Small wind turbines offer a practical solution for individual homes or communities in suitable areas, with considerations for initial costs, maintenance, and the benefits of renewable, clean electricity.
- Hydropower, especially micro-hydro systems, is discussed for its continuous power supply

capability. Site selection and DIY options are explored for off-grid living and emergency preparedness.

- Manual power generation techniques, including hand crank generators, bicycle generators, and manual treadmills, are explored as vital for resilience and self-sufficiency in grid-down scenarios.
- Battery storage and management are critical for maintaining a reliable energy supply, with details on different battery types, storage best practices, and the importance of a Battery Management System (BMS).
- Creating a renewable energy plan involves assessing energy needs, exploring renewable options like solar, wind, and hydropower, integrating with battery storage, and ensuring system maintenance and redundancy for grid-down resilience.

6
COMMUNICATION AND NAVIGATION

Basic Signaling Techniques

When the grid goes down, traditional communication methods may fail, making it essential to revert to basic signaling techniques for conveying messages or attracting attention in emergencies. These methods are crucial for survival, finding help, or indicating your location. Visual signals are straightforward, ranging from creating smoke during the day to using mirrors or reflective surfaces to catch sunlight. Smoke signals are produced by starting a fire and covering it with green vegetation to generate smoke, ensuring the smoke contrasts with the background. Mirrors or reflective surfaces can be used to flash sunlight in a specific direction, requiring practice to aim accurately.

Sound signals become more effective when visibility is poor, or distances are great. These can include blowing a whistle, banging metal objects together, or using a horn to create a noise distinct from natural background sounds. Especially useful in dense forests or at night, the universal distress signal involves three blasts of sound, such as three whistle blows or three gunshots, repeated every few minutes to enhance the chances of being heard. Additionally, marking your path when moving through unfamiliar territory or needing to retrace your steps is vital. This can be achieved by tying fabric to branches, stacking rocks, or marking trees with chalk or charcoal, ensuring these markers are noticeable and consistent.

Nature also offers indicators for navigation, such as moss growing on the northern side of trees in the northern hemisphere or using the position of the sun and stars for guidance. Reading these natural signs is invaluable when other navigation aids are unavailable. While these signaling techniques may seem simple, practice dramatically enhances their effectiveness. Familiarizing yourself with these methods before they are needed ensures efficient and effective use in survival situations, with regular practice sessions refining these skills. In conclusion, mastering basic signaling techniques is fundamental to survival in a grid-down scenario, enabling communication over distances, attracting attention in emergencies, and navigating unfamiliar territories, significantly increasing your chances of survival and rescue.

Using Radios for Communication

Maintaining communication with your group or reaching out for help is crucial in a grid-down scenario. With conventional communication means like cell phones and the internet unavailable, radios become an essential lifeline. This section explores the practical use of radios for communication, focusing on different types, operations, and best practices to ensure connectivity during crises.

Handheld radios or walkie-talkies are compact and user-friendly for short-range communication within a group. They operate on various frequencies, including the Family Radio Service (FRS) and General Mobile Radio Service (GMRS) bands. FRS radios are accessible without a license and suitable for general use. GMRS radios, offering a longer range, require a license from the Federal Communications Commission (FCC) in the United States.

Ham radios are unmatched for long-distance communication. They can operate on multiple frequencies, enabling communication across towns, states, or even internationally under certain conditions. However, using a ham radio requires a license obtained by passing an exam that covers radio theory, operating practices, and regulations. Citizen Band (CB) radios also provide short-to-medium-range communication without a license. Truckers commonly use them, making them a valuable tool for survival communication.

Ensure your radios have a reliable power source, such as

AA or AAA batteries or rechargeable battery packs. Consider solar or hand-crank chargers to keep your radios operational when traditional power sources fail. Understanding the frequencies your radio can access and any legal restrictions is also essential. Privacy can be a concern since others can listen to your communications, use privacy codes if available, and be cautious about the information you share.

The range of your radio can be significantly affected by its antenna. In some cases, upgrading to a higher-quality antenna or setting up a base station with an external antenna for ham radios can significantly extend your reach. Establish clear communication protocols within your group, use call signs to identify each member, and agree on specific frequencies and times for check-ins. Keep transmissions brief and to the point to conserve battery life and minimize the chance of interception.

Familiarize yourself with your radio equipment and practice using it regularly to ensure efficient operation in an emergency. Maintain radio discipline by transmitting only when necessary and keeping communications concise to conserve battery life and maintain operational security. Develop a comprehensive communication plan that includes primary and secondary frequencies, rendezvous points, and protocols for message passing, ensuring every group member understands and can execute the plan.

In conclusion, radios are vital tools for communication in a grid-down situation. By selecting the appropriate type of radio, understanding its operation, and adhering to best practices, you can maintain a lifeline between your group and the outside world, even when other forms of communication are unavailable.

Navigating Without GPS

Reliance on technology, especially GPS for navigation, has become second nature in the modern world. However, in a grid-down scenario, these conveniences may no longer be available, necessitating a return to more traditional methods of finding one's way. This section delves into the essential skills and knowledge required to navigate without GPS, ensuring you can confidently move from point A to point B without needing electronic devices.

The foundation of navigation without GPS lies in understanding the basic principles of direction and location. Your primary guides are the cardinal directions—north, south, east, and west. Familiarizing yourself with the sun's position at different times of the day can provide a rudimentary method of determining direction. Remember, the sun rises in the east and sets in the west. At noon, when the sun is at its highest point, it will be directly south in the Northern Hemisphere and north in the Southern Hemisphere.

Nature provides an abundance of indicators that can help in navigation. For instance, moss often grows on the northern side of trees in the Northern Hemisphere due to reduced exposure to sunlight. Similarly, observing the stars can be a reliable method for night-time navigation. The North Star,

Polaris, remains relatively fixed in the sky and indicates true north. Learning to recognize constellations such as the Big Dipper, which points towards Polaris, can be invaluable.

Creating an improvised compass is a practical skill when traditional navigation tools are unavailable. One method involves using a needle, magnetizing it by rubbing it against silk or wool and then floating it on a leaf in a water bowl. The needle will align with the Earth's magnetic field, pointing towards the magnetic north. While this method may not be as accurate as a standard compass, it can provide a general sense of direction.

Identifying and using landmarks is a crucial skill in navigation without GPS. Natural landmarks such as mountains, rivers, distinctive rock formations, and artificial structures can serve as points of reference to maintain orientation and track progress. Wayfinding involves choosing landmarks in the direction of travel and moving from one to the next, ensuring that you stay on course.

Developing the ability to create mental maps of your surroundings is essential for navigation without electronic aids. This involves paying close attention to the environment and noting changes in terrain, vegetation, and other features. Keeping a mental note of the direction and distance traveled from known points can help maintain a sense of location and direction.

In conclusion, while the absence of GPS and other electronic navigation aids in a grid-down scenario may initially seem daunting, navigating effectively using traditional methods is possible. You can confidently find your way in any environment by understanding basic navigation principles, utilizing natural indicators, improvising tools, and developing keen observation skills.

Map Reading and Land Navigation

When GPS and digital maps are unavailable, the ability to read a map and navigate the land becomes invaluable. This section equips you with the knowledge to find your way in an uncertain world. A map is more than just a piece of paper; it's a scaled-down representation of the Earth's surface. The first step in mastering map reading is to familiarize yourself with the map's scale, legend, and symbols. The scale indicates the relationship between distances on the map and the actual distances on the ground. At the same time, the legend, or key, deciphers the symbols and colors used on the map, representing various physical features such as rivers, roads, and terrain types.

To use a map effectively, you must orient it to the surrounding environment by aligning the map so that its north corresponds with true north or magnetic north, which can be done using a compass or by identifying landmarks. A compass is an essential tool for navigation, especially when traversing unfamiliar terrain. It points toward magnetic north, which, combined with a correctly oriented map, allows you to determine your direction of travel. Maps also depict terrain features that can help or hinder your movement, including contours, vegetation, water bodies, and artificial structures. Learning to read these features enables you to choose the best path of travel and anticipate potential challenges.

Once you've oriented your map and identified your current location and destination, the next step is to plot a course by determining the direction and distance between the two points. Consider natural obstacles and terrain features that may require detours, use the map's scale to estimate distances, and plan your route accordingly. Pacing and dead reckoning help you navigate without landmarks by counting steps to estimate the distance traveled and navigating from a known position to a new one using estimated speeds, elapsed time, and bearing. These methods require practice to develop accuracy but can be invaluable in featureless terrain.

The key to successful navigation is knowing how to find your way and avoid getting lost. Always keep track of your position on the map, check against landmarks regularly, and adjust your course as needed. If you are disoriented, stop, reassess your location using the map and compass, and retrace your steps if necessary. You can confidently navigate the landscape in a grid-down scenario by understanding the basics, orienting the map, using a compass, recognizing terrain features, plotting a course, and employing pacing and dead reckoning. Remember, the key to effective navigation is practice; the more you use these skills, the more proficient you will become.

Creating and Using Codes

Effective communication becomes paramount in a grid-down scenario where conventional means might be compromised, monitored, or unavailable. This necessitates the development of alternative methods to convey messages securely, such as creating and using codes. Codes are a powerful tool for maintaining privacy and ensuring that critical information is shared only with intended recipients.

The first step in creating a code is to decide on the type that best suits your needs. Simple substitution codes can be effective for basic messages. At the same time, more sophisticated methods like the Vigenère cipher are suitable for complex or sensitive information. The code must be complex enough to deter unintended deciphering but simple enough for all intended recipients to understand and use without confusion.

Codes can be used to encode locations of supply caches, detail rendezvous points, or convey status updates and requests for assistance. They can be transmitted through written notes, discreet signals, or digitally if some electronic communication remains operational. Practicing encoding and decoding messages with your group is crucial to ensure proficiency and identify potential issues with the code system.

The effectiveness of a code can diminish over time, especially if there's a risk it has been compromised. Protocols for regularly updating or changing codes are essential, which might involve setting predetermined intervals for changes or implementing a system to trigger an immediate change if there's suspicion of compromise.

Without conventional communication methods, codes offer a secure alternative for conveying important information. By carefully creating and practicing codes, you can enhance your group's ability to communicate effectively and securely in a grid-down environment. The goal is to prevent outsiders from understanding your messages and ensure that your team can communicate efficiently under stress and in challenging conditions. Maintaining operational security will be our next focus, building on the foundation of secure communication established through effective coding practices.

Maintaining Operational Security

Maintaining operational security (OPSEC) is important, especially when it comes to communication and navigation. In this context, OPSEC refers to the measures and protocols you put in place to prevent unauthorized access to your plans, movements, and communications. It ensures that sensitive information remains within your trusted circle, safeguarding you and your group from potential threats.

It's crucial to understand that every piece of information, no matter how trivial it might seem, could be valuable to someone with malicious intent. Therefore, the first step in maintaining operational security is identifying sensitive information and limiting its exposure. This includes details about your location, resources, routes, and communication methods.

When discussing sensitive information, do so in a secure environment. Avoid open spaces or areas where you could be easily overheard. If you're using electronic devices, ensure they are secure and protected against unauthorized access. This might involve encrypting your communications or using secure, dedicated channels for sensitive discussions.

Another key aspect of OPSEC is being aware of your surroundings and understanding that information can be inadvertently leaked through non-verbal cues. For instance, packing your vehicle in a manner that suggests you're leaving for an extended period could attract unwanted attention. Similarly, a sudden change in your daily routine might signal to observant eyes that something is amiss. Be mindful of these non-verbal cues and strive to maintain a low profile.

Regarding navigation, operational security means moving discreetly and avoiding predictable patterns. If you need to scout or travel, do so at times and through routes that minimize your visibility and exposure. Vary your routes and schedules to avoid establishing patterns that could be easily tracked.

Communication discipline is also a critical component of OPSEC. This involves knowing when to communicate and what medium to use. For instance, radio communications should be kept brief, encrypted, and only used when necessary. The same principle applies to any form of electronic communication. Always assume that your communications could be intercepted and plan accordingly.

Lastly, trust is a cornerstone of operational security. Be cautious about who you share sensitive information with. Even within your group, operate on a need-to-know basis. The fewer people who know the details of your plans and movements, the less likely it is for that information to fall into the wrong hands.

In summary, maintaining operational security in a grid-down scenario requires vigilance, discipline, and a thorough understanding of the potential risks associated with communication and navigation. By implementing these principles, you can significantly reduce your vulnerability and enhance your chances of safely navigating challenging times.

Chapter Summary

- Basic survival signaling techniques include visual signals (e.g., smoke, mirrors), sound signals, trail marking, and using natural navigation indicators.
- Regularly practicing signaling methods improves effectiveness, aiding long-distance communication, emergency attention, and navigation.
- Radios (handheld, ham, CB) are crucial in grid-down scenarios; knowledge of their operation, power sources, and privacy is necessary.

- Effective radio use requires understanding frequencies, enhancing range with antennas, establishing protocols, and practicing discipline for security and battery conservation.
- Navigating without GPS involves mastering natural indicators, improvising tools like compasses, and honing observation skills.
- Map reading and land navigation require understanding map fundamentals, compass use, recognizing terrain, and employing pacing and dead reckoning techniques.
- Creating and using codes for secure communication in grid-down scenarios is essential, emphasizing clarity, simplicity, and regular updates.
- Maintaining operational security (OPSEC) includes protecting sensitive information, practicing discreet communication and movement, avoiding predictability, and limiting information sharing.

7
SURVIVAL GEAR AND TOOLS

Essential Survival Gear

In grid-down survival, a well-curated selection of essential survival gear forms the backbone of your survival strategy, enabling you to navigate, sustain, and protect yourself in an environment stripped of modern conveniences and services. The following items are considered indispensable for anyone preparing for a failed grid scenario.

Water Filtration and Purification Devices: Access to clean drinking water is paramount. In the absence of tap water, you must have the means to purify natural water sources. Portable water filters, purification tablets, or a simple boiling setup can make the difference between hydration and dehydration, health, and illness.

Durable Multi-Tool and Fixed-Blade Knife: A high-quality multi-tool can perform numerous tasks, from repairing gear to preparing food. Complement this with a sturdy fixed-blade knife, invaluable for heavier tasks such as chopping wood or building shelter.

Fire Starting Tools: The ability to start a fire is critical for warmth, cooking, and morale. Your kit should include waterproof matches, ferro rods, and lighters. Practice using these tools in various conditions to ensure you can reliably produce fire when needed.

First Aid Kit: A comprehensive kit tailored to your group's specific needs and any known medical conditions is essential. Beyond the basics, include prescription medications, a tourniquet, and trauma shears. Knowledge of first aid practices is equally important, so consider taking courses to enhance your skills.

Shelter and Warmth Items: Exposure to the elements can be life-threatening. Compact, lightweight options such as emergency bivvy bags, tarps, and space blankets can provide immediate shelter and help retain body heat.

Light Sources: Reliable light sources such as headlamps, flashlights, and lanterns, along with an ample supply of batteries or alternative charging methods (solar, hand-crank), are crucial. These tools aid in navigation and camp setup and can signal for help in emergencies.

Communication Devices: Traditional communication methods may be unavailable in a grid-down scenario. Hand-crank or solar-powered radios can receive weather and news updates, while two-way radios can facilitate communication with your group or nearby allies.

Navigation Tools: GPS devices may be unreliable or unavailable, making traditional navigation tools like maps and compasses indispensable. Familiarize yourself with their use and keep local and regional maps in your kit.

Food Supplies: While long-term food storage is a broader topic, your immediate survival gear should include high-calorie, nutrient-dense foods that require minimal preparation, such as energy bars, nuts, and ready-to-eat meals.

Personal Hygiene Items: Maintaining personal hygiene prevents infections and diseases. Include items such as hand sanitizer, soap, toothbrush, and toothpaste, along with a small towel.

Each item in your survival gear must be carefully chosen, considering its utility, durability, and weight. Regularly review and maintain your gear, ensuring everything is in working order, and consumables are within their use-by dates. Familiarity with your equipment is as crucial as the gear itself; practice using each item in various conditions to ensure you can rely on it when the situation demands.

Choosing and Maintaining Tools

In grid-down survival, the importance of selecting the right tools cannot be overstated. These tools need to be durable and versatile and also maintainable with limited resources. The process of choosing and maintaining your survival tools is a critical skill that can significantly impact your ability to navigate challenging times.

When selecting tools, prioritize those made from high-quality materials. Stainless steel, for example, is renowned for its rust resistance and overall durability, making it an excellent choice for knives, multi-tools, and other gear. However, it's also essential to consider the tool's weight and size, as you may need to transport your gear over long distances. Opt for tools that offer multiple functions in a single design to reduce the need to carry extra items.

After choosing your tools, the next crucial step is familiarizing yourself with their proper maintenance. Regular cleaning and sharpening can significantly extend the life of your tools. For instance, a knife should be cleaned after each use and sharpened regularly to ensure it remains effective for cutting and carving tasks. Learning to sharpen your tools with a whetstone or sharpening rod is a valuable skill that will serve you well.

Rust prevention is another critical aspect of tool maintenance. Applying a light coat of oil to metal parts can prevent rust and corrosion, especially in humid environments. Be sure to use an oil safe for all your tools' materials, including any handles made from wood or synthetic materials.

Storage plays a significant role in maintaining the condition of your tools. Tools should be stored in a dry, clean place to prevent damage when not in use. If you're on the move, consider using protective sheaths or cases to safeguard your tools from the elements and accidental damage.

Lastly, it's worth noting that the ability to repair your tools can be just as important as maintaining them. Familiarize yourself with common repair techniques, such as replacing tool handles or tightening loose components. A basic repair kit that includes items like screws, nuts, bolts, and adhesives can be invaluable in extending the life of your tools.

In conclusion, selecting and maintaining your survival tools are foundational aspects of preparedness for a grid-down scenario. By choosing durable, versatile tools and committing to their regular maintenance and repair, you can ensure that your gear remains reliable and effective, no matter the challenges you face.

DIY Survival Tools

The ability to adapt and create your tools from available resources can be a game-changer. This section delves into the world of DIY survival tools, offering practical advice on how to craft essential gear using minimal resources. The focus here is on creating tools from scratch and repurposing and improvising with what you have, ensuring you remain resilient and resourceful in the face of adversity.

A knife is one of the most versatile tools in any survival situation. Creating a basic survival knife from natural materials can be your first DIY project if you find yourself without one. Look for a piece of flint or obsidian for the blade, which can be knapped or chipped away to create a sharp edge. A sturdy piece of wood secured to the stone blade with strips of leather, cloth, or even strong plant fibers will suffice for the handle.

Securing food is a priority in survival situations, and fish can be an excellent source of nutrition. A fishing spear can be made by selecting a long, straight branch of hardwood, sharpening one end into a point, or splitting the end into four prongs and sharpening each for a more effective tool. Heating the points over a fire can harden them, making your spear more durable and significantly increasing your chances of catching fish in shallow water.

Clean water is crucial, and knowing how to construct a basic filtration system can save your life—using a container, such as a bottle with the bottom cut off, layer charcoal from your fire, sand, and small stones. Pouring water through this makeshift filter can remove significant particulates and improve water quality before boiling or purification. However, this method doesn't purify water; it is a preliminary step to remove larger debris.

Your ability to construct a shelter from natural materials can protect you from the elements and improve your chances of survival. A simple lean-to can be made by leaning branches against a fallen tree or rock, creating a frame, and covering this frame with smaller branches, leaves, and debris for insulation and protection from wind and rain. The key is creating a space that retains heat and protects you from the environment.

Fire is essential for warmth, cooking, and morale. Without matches or a lighter, creating a fire using friction is a primitive but effective method. The bow drill method, which involves rapidly spinning a wooden spindle against a fireboard to create an ember, is one of the most efficient friction-fire techniques. It requires patience and practice but ensures you can create fire without modern conveniences.

Crafting DIY survival tools is an invaluable skill in any grid-down scenario. These examples are just the beginning. With creativity and resourcefulness, almost anything can be repurposed into a useful tool. Remember, the key to survival is not just your gear but your knowledge and ingenuity in using what's available to you. As we move forward, we'll explore how everyday items can be transformed into multi-use survival tools, further expanding your ability to adapt and thrive in any situation.

Multi-Use Items for Survival

In grid-down survival, the efficiency of your gear can mean the difference between thriving and merely surviving. This section delves into the critical importance of multi-use items in your survival toolkit, emphasizing their role in ensuring you're well-prepared for various scenarios without overburdening your pack.

One of the quintessential multi-use items is the paracord. Known for its strength and versatility, paracord can secure shelters, repair gear, fish, set traps, and even be a makeshift tourniquet. Its lightweight nature and the ability to unravel it into thinner strands make it indispensable in any survival situation.

Another invaluable multi-use tool is the bandana. Beyond its primary use as headwear to protect against the sun, a bandana can serve as a filter for water before purification, a sling for injured limbs, a signal flag, and even a tinder for starting fires. Its compact size allows multiple bandanas to be easily carried without taking up significant space.

The multi-tool, embodying the essence of versatility, is a must-have for any survival kit. With various built-in tools such as pliers, knives, screwdrivers, and can openers, a sturdy multi-tool can tackle many tasks, from gear repair to food preparation. Opting for a high-quality multi-tool ensures durability and reliability when needed.

A stainless steel water bottle offers more than just hydration. When empty, it can boil water, making it safe to drink or cook simple meals. Stainless steel's durability also means it can withstand the rigors of outdoor survival situations, providing a reliable container for water storage and more.

Lastly, duct tape's reputation for fixing nearly anything holds true in survival scenarios. Its uses are only limited by one's creativity, including repairing gear, sealing containers, making emergency bandages, and even crafting makeshift shoes. A roll of duct tape takes up minimal space but offers endless utility.

Incorporating these multi-use items into your survival gear maximizes the utility of each item carried and significantly reduces the weight and bulk of your pack. This approach to selecting gear ensures you're prepared for various challenges, making your survival strategy efficient and effective.

As we transition from crafting and improvisation of DIY survival tools, understanding the significance of multi-use items sets a solid foundation for the next step: packaging and transporting your gear. Packing smartly and prioritizing items that serve multiple purposes is crucial in maintaining mobility and readiness in any grid-down scenario.

Packaging and Transporting Gear

How you package and transport your gear can significantly impact your mobility, efficiency, and, ultimately, your survival. This section delves into the essential considerations and strategies for effectively packaging and transporting your survival gear, ensuring that you remain agile and prepared.

Choosing the Right Containers: The first step in effectively packaging your gear is selecting the right containers. Waterproof, durable, and lightweight containers are ideal. Dry bags, for instance, offer an excellent solution for keeping your items dry and can be easily compressed to save space. Hard cases, while heavier, provide unmatched protection for delicate equipment such as communication devices or medical supplies. When selecting containers, consider the nature of the items you're packing and the conditions you expect to encounter.

Compartmentalization: Organizing your gear into categories and packing it into separate compartments or bags within your main pack can save precious time when you need to access specific items quickly. Use color-coded bags or labels to easily identify the contents without having to unpack everything. This method not only streamlines access but also helps maintain an inventory of your supplies.

Weight Distribution: Proper weight distribution is crucial when packing your gear, especially if carrying it on your back for extended periods. Heavy items should be packed closer to your body and in the middle of the pack to maintain balance and reduce strain. Lighter items can be placed on the outside or in external pockets. Testing the pack's weight and adjusting the distribution can prevent fatigue and injury.

Modularity: Adopting a modular approach to packing your gear can offer flexibility and adaptability in various scenarios. Modular packing involves grouping items into separate modules or kits based on their function (e.g., fire-starting, first-aid, food kit). This strategy allows you to quickly adapt to changing conditions by reconfiguring the modules you carry without repacking your entire gear.

Transport Methods: The method of transporting your gear will largely depend on the terrain, distance, and your physical condition. While backpacks are the most common choice for hands-free convenience, alternative methods such as carts, sleds, or even pack animals may be more suitable in certain situations. Each method has advantages and limitations, and choosing the right one can significantly enhance mobility and efficiency.

Practice and Preparedness: Finally, the best-laid plans for packaging and transporting gear can only be validated through practice. Regularly packing, carrying, and accessing your gear in a controlled environment can reveal shortcomings in your strategy and provide valuable insights for improvement. Additionally, practicing with your gear in various weather conditions and terrains can prepare you for the unpredictability of real-world scenarios.

In conclusion, how you package and transport your survival gear is critical to your preparedness strategy. By choosing suitable containers, compartmentalizing your supplies, focusing on weight distribution, adopting a modular approach, selecting the appropriate transport method, and practicing regularly, you can ensure that your gear enhances rather than hinders your survival capabilities.

Innovative Uses for Common Items

This section delves into innovative uses for everyday objects, transforming them into essential survival gear. The focus is not just on what to pack but on seeing the potential in what you already have.

Dental floss, often overlooked as merely a dental hygiene tool, is a strong and versatile thread perfect for survival. It can be used as a fishing line, a snare for small game, or to tie together shelter materials, making it an invaluable addition to any survival kit due to its strength and compact size. Plastic bottles, another common item, can be repurposed in numerous ways, such as containers for collecting water or makeshift scoops. When filled with water and left in the sun, clear plastic bottles can purify water through solar water disinfection, and they also serve as waterproof containers for storing sensitive items like matches or tinder.

Aluminum foil is a multifunctional material that is lightweight, compact, and moldable, ideal for survival scenarios. It can be used to cook food, create makeshift bowls, or enhance the fire signal by reflecting light, and in emergencies, it can be molded into a cutting tool or used as insulation. Sanitary pads and tampons, typically used for personal care, also have several survival applications; pads are highly absorbent and can be used as dressings for large wounds, while both can be used as fire-starting fuel or to filter debris from the water.

Eyeglasses can double as a tool for starting fires in sunny conditions by focusing sunlight onto a small point, similar to a magnifying glass. While requiring patience and precise angling, this method can be crucial when traditional fire-starting tools are unavailable. Steel wool, a common household item, also has unexpected survival uses; when touched by the terminals of a battery, it can ignite, providing a quick way to start a fire. It is also helpful for cleaning tools or making emergency repairs.

The ability to repurpose everyday items for survival enhances preparedness, saves space in your survival kit, and encourages creative problem-solving in challenging situations. By viewing everyday items through the lens of survival, you equip yourself with a versatile toolkit adaptable to various scenarios, significantly boosting your survival capabilities.

Chapter Summary

- Essential survival gear includes water filtration devices, multi-tools, fire-starting tools, first aid kits, shelter and warmth items, light sources, communication devices, navigation tools, food supplies, and personal hygiene items.
- Selecting and maintaining tools is crucial in a grid-down scenario, emphasizing the importance of durability, versatility, and the ability to maintain them with limited resources.
- DIY survival tools, such as a basic survival knife, fishing spear, water filter, shelter, and fire-making techniques, can be crafted from natural or available materials, enhancing adaptability and resourcefulness.
- Multi-use items like paracord, bandanas, multi-tools, stainless steel water bottles, and duct tape

are emphasized for their versatility and efficiency in survival situations.
- Effective packaging and transporting of gear involve choosing suitable containers, compartmentalization, proper weight distribution, modularity, selecting appropriate transport methods, and regular practice.
- Innovative uses for everyday items, such as dental floss for fishing lines, plastic bottles for water purification, aluminum foil for cooking, sanitary pads and tampons for wound care and fire starting, eyeglasses for fire starting, and steel wool for fire starting and repairs, showcase adaptability.
- The importance of creativity and ingenuity in using everyday items for survival purposes is highlighted, encouraging a mindset of seeing potential in common objects for various survival applications.
- The text underscores the significance of preparedness, knowledge, and the ability to adapt and improvise with specialized gear and everyday items in a grid-down scenario.

8
SELF-DEFENSE AND TACTICAL TRAINING

Basic Self-Defense Techniques

Knowing how to defend oneself is crucial in a grid-down scenario where societal norms may collapse. Self-defense encompasses a range of skills, from situational awareness to understanding legal implications. Still, we focus on basic techniques accessible to individuals of all fitness levels. These methods are practical, effective, and designed for quick learning, setting the groundwork for more advanced skills.

Understanding foundational self-defense principles is essential. The primary objective is to avoid confrontations, using de-escalation and evasion as first-line strategies. However, knowing how to protect oneself is vital when conflict is unavoidable.

A proper stance is fundamental in self-defense, providing

stability, mobility, and readiness. Position your feet shoulder-width apart, one slightly ahead, with knees slightly bent. This stance allows for quick movements and helps maintain balance during physical confrontations.

Effective striking involves knowing which body parts can serve as weapons and targeting vulnerable areas of an attacker, such as the eyes, nose, throat, and groin. Use the heel of your palm, elbows, knees, and feet to deliver powerful strikes, aiming to incapacitate the attacker long enough to escape.

Blocking or parrying attacks helps avoid taking damage. Keep your hands up to protect your face and neck, using your arms to deflect blows. Observing the attacker's movements and reacting swiftly is crucial for effective defense.

If an attacker grabs you, knowing how to break free is crucial. Techniques depend on the nature of the hold but generally involve using leverage and quick movements to escape. For instance, twisting against an attacker's thumb when they grab your wrist can break their grip.

When defending yourself on the ground, protect your vital areas and use your legs to fend off attackers. Practice getting up quickly and safely, as being on the ground is a significant disadvantage.

Proficiency in these techniques requires practice. Enrolling in a self-defense class offers the opportunity to learn from experienced instructors and build the muscle memory needed for effective response under stress.

The ultimate goal of self-defense is personal safety and

the protection of others. It's about preparation, awareness, and appropriate reaction in crises. Individuals can develop a comprehensive self-defense strategy tailored to their abilities and needs with these basic techniques.

Firearms Training and Safety

While basic self-defense techniques provide a foundation, introducing firearms into one's survival strategy significantly increases defensive capability and requires a complex set of responsibilities and skills. Firearms training and safety are critical components of self-defense and tactical training, requiring careful consideration and continuous practice.

First and foremost, understanding and respecting the fundamental rules of firearm safety is non-negotiable. These rules include treating every firearm as if it is loaded, never pointing a firearm at anything you are not willing to destroy, keeping your finger off the trigger until you are ready to shoot, and being aware of your target and what is beyond it. These principles form the bedrock of safe firearm handling and are applicable in every situation, whether in a controlled training environment or the unpredictability of a grid-down scenario.

Beyond basic safety, selecting the right firearm is a critical decision. Factors to consider include the firearm's purpose (self-defense, hunting, or perimeter security), the shooter's proficiency and comfort with the firearm, and the availability of ammunition. For many, a versatile and reliable rifle or shotgun, combined with a handgun for personal defense, provides a balanced approach. However, the specific choice should be tailored to the individual's situation and needs.

Training is where the theoretical knowledge of firearms safety and the practical shooting skills converge. Effective firearms training encompasses marksmanship, situational awareness, stress management, and decision-making under pressure. Regular practice at a shooting range can build proficiency, but scenario-based training exercises that simulate potential real-life situations are invaluable. These exercises help to prepare for the psychological and physiological effects of a high-stress encounter, teaching the shooter to maintain focus, make rapid decisions, and accurately deploy their firearm when necessary.

Maintenance and care of firearms are as crucial as the skills to use them. A well-maintained firearm is reliable, safe, and effective. This includes regular cleaning, proper storage, and the timely replacement of worn parts. Understanding the mechanical aspects of one's firearms ensures they function as expected when needed most.

Lastly, the legal and ethical considerations of using firearms for self-defense cannot be overstressed. Even in a grid-down scenario, the principles of lawful self-defense remain relevant. Lethal force is a grave responsibility and should always be considered a last resort. Understanding the legal framework surrounding self-defense and firearms use in one's jurisdiction before a crisis occurs is essential.

As we transition from the foundational aspects of firearms training and safety to the innovative realm of improvised weapons and tools, it's clear that self-defense in a grid-down world is multifaceted. Firearms play a critical role but are part of a broader strategy that includes a wide range of skills and considerations. The goal is always to ensure the safety and security of oneself and one's community through preparedness, training, and the ethical use of force.

Improvised Weapons and Tools

Mastering improvised weapons and tools is essential for survival in a grid-down scenario. Almost any object can be transformed into a means of self-defense if used with skill and determination. It's essential to evaluate items for their typical uses and potential in a survival context, considering factors like weight, balance, and durability.

Everyday items such as pens, pencils, keys, bottles, ropes, flashlights, and belts can all be repurposed as weapons. For instance, pens and pencils can be used for stabbing, keys can enhance the impact of a punch, and belts can serve as whips or binding tools. Additionally, creating tools is equally crucial; broken glass or sharp stones can serve as cutting tools, while boards or flat stones can be used for digging.

Training and practice are vital to utilize these improvised weapons and tools effectively. Understanding basic striking, cutting, and defensive techniques enhances proficiency. It's also important to consider any weapon's ethical and legal implications. These skills should only be used in self-defense to ensure safety and de-escalate conflicts. Integrating these principles into your survival strategy prepares you for emergencies and bolsters your adaptability and resourcefulness.

Tactical Movement and Camouflage

Moving stealthily and remaining undetected in a grid-down scenario are as crucial as self-defense skills. Tactical movement and camouflage are vital for navigating hostile environments while minimizing confrontation risks. This guide provides practical advice on blending into surroundings and moving without drawing attention.

Tactical movement involves efficiently transitioning from one location to another with minimal exposure. Fundamental principles include minimizing noise, avoiding silhouetting, using natural and artificial cover, and moving slowly and deliberately. To minimize noise, move slowly to reduce the sound of footsteps, wear soft-soled shoes, and avoid stepping on noisy underbrush.

Avoid silhouetting by being mindful of your background and moving through areas where your outline blends with the surroundings rather than open spaces. Differentiate between cover, which protects from projectiles, and concealment, which hides you from view, using both strategically. Rapid movements attract attention, so move slowly, pause often to observe and listen, and prioritize stealth over speed.

Camouflage involves using clothing, materials, and techniques to blend into the environment, making you less visible. Effective camouflage requires understanding how to manage shape, shine, shadow, silhouette, and spacing. Wear patterned clothing that mimics the environment and add natural elements to disrupt your outline. Cover or remove shiny objects, and be mindful of your shadow, especially in low light.

In addition to visual camouflage, securing loose gear minimizes odors and controls noise. Like any skill, effective camouflage requires practice. Spend time in various environments to observe how well you blend in and adjust your techniques accordingly.

Mastering tactical movement and camouflage improves your ability to navigate a grid-down world safely, enhancing your chances of avoiding confrontations and providing a strategic advantage where stealth is key to survival. The goal is to avoid detection, preserve safety, and conserve resources when necessary.

Situational Awareness and Threat Assessment

In grid-down survival, accurately assessing your surroundings and identifying potential threats before they become imminent dangers is an invaluable skill. This section delves into the critical concepts of situational awareness and threat assessment, providing the knowledge and techniques necessary to enhance your safety and security in uncertain times.

Situational awareness is the practice of being mindful of your environment and understanding what is happening around you at all times. It involves continuously observing the people, objects, and events in your vicinity and interpreting their significance for your safety. To develop situational awareness, start by honing your observational skills. Make a habit of scanning your environment, noting exits, potential hazards, and the behavior of individuals nearby. It's essential to remain discreet and avoid tunnel vision; focus on the big picture rather than fixating on a single element.

Another critical aspect of situational awareness is understanding baseline behaviors for the environments you frequent. Baselines are the norms or averages of behavior and conditions in a specific area. By recognizing when something deviates from the baseline, you can quickly identify potential threats. For example, an abrupt silence or a sudden gathering of people in a typically bustling market may indicate a problem or threat. Learning to detect these anomalies allows you to react swiftly and appropriately.

Threat assessment is identifying and evaluating potential threats to determine their severity and likelihood of becoming actual dangers. This involves recognizing immediate threats and anticipating future ones based on the information at hand. Effective threat assessment requires a combination of intuition, experience, and logical analysis. Start by categorizing potential threats based on their nature—human, environmental, or technological. Then, evaluate each threat based on its capability to harm you, its opportunity to do so, and its intent. This triad will help you prioritize which threats need immediate attention and which can be monitored or mitigated.

Incorporating situational awareness and threat assessment into your daily routine may seem daunting initially, but it becomes second nature with practice. Begin by consciously applying these principles in safe, familiar environments and gradually expand to more complex scenarios. Training exercises, such as scenario planning and role-playing, can also be beneficial in developing these skills. Remember, the goal is not to live in a state of paranoia but to cultivate a heightened awareness that empowers you to make informed decisions and take proactive measures to protect yourself and your loved ones.

By mastering situational awareness and threat assessment, you equip yourself with the tools necessary to navigate the unpredictable landscape of a grid-down scenario. These skills enhance your ability to avoid or mitigate dangers and contribute to the overall resilience and security of your survival strategy. As we progress, the emphasis will shift towards leveraging these individual skills to foster collective strength and security by building a cohesive survival team.

Building a Survival Team

Understanding the formation and structuring of a survival team is crucial. Ideally, this team acts as a cohesive unit capable of defending, providing for, and supporting each other during societal collapse. It's not just about gathering individuals; it's about assembling a team with complementary skills, a shared commitment to survival, and the ability to operate under stress with trust and efficiency.

The composition of your survival team is paramount and should include individuals with various essential skills. These skills include medical knowledge, self-defense and tactical training, food production and preservation, mechanical repair, and communication. Each member should bring a unique set of skills to the table, ensuring the team can address various challenges.

Trust and reliability form the bedrock of any effective survival team. Members must be able to rely on each other implicitly, as the stakes in a grid-down scenario are incredibly high. This trust is built over time through training, shared experiences, and developing interpersonal relationships. It's crucial to vet potential team members thoroughly.

Training together is an essential aspect of building a cohesive survival team. Regular, structured training sessions in self-defense, first aid, emergency communication, and other survival skills are crucial. These sessions improve individual and group proficiency and enhance team bonding and trust. Training scenarios should be as realistic as possible to prepare the team for a grid-down environment's physical and psychological challenges.

Leadership within the survival team should be clear yet flexible. While a designated leader can provide direction and make critical decisions, a rigid hierarchy can stifle initiative and adaptability. Leadership might rotate based on the situation or the specific skills required at the time, and decision-making should balance leveraging the leader's expertise with incorporating input from team members.

Effective communication is vital for a survival team's success. This includes tactical communication during operations and regular discussions about plans, challenges, and group dynamics. Conflict is inevitable in high-stress situations; therefore, the team must have strategies in place for conflict resolution, including mediation and structured discussions.

Finally, a survival team must be committed to continuous improvement. This means regularly reviewing and critiquing performance, learning from successes and failures, and staying informed about new survival strategies and technologies. The landscape of a grid-down scenario is ever-changing, and adaptability is critical to long-term survival. Building a survival team is a complex but crucial process that requires careful consideration of skills, trust, leadership, and continuous improvement. This will enhance the chances of survival and provide a support system that can make the ordeal psychologically bearable.

Chapter Summary

- Basic self-defense techniques are crucial in scenarios where society's structure collapses. They focus on practical, effective methods suitable for individuals of varying physical fitness.
- Foundational self-defense principles include avoiding confrontation, adopting a stable and ready stance, effective striking using body parts less prone to injury, and targeting vulnerable areas on an attacker.
- Techniques for blocking, parrying, breaking away from grabs, and ground defense are essential, with emphasis on leverage, swift movements, and protecting vital organs.
- Regular training and practice under experienced instructors are recommended to build proficiency and muscle memory for effective self-defense under stress.
- Firearms training and safety are critical, emphasizing respect for fundamental safety rules, selecting appropriate firearms, and continuous practice for skill proficiency and maintenance.
- Improvised weapons and tools from everyday items can be vital in self-defense, with training enhancing their effectiveness. Ethical and legal considerations remain paramount.

- Tactical movement and camouflage skills are essential for stealth and avoiding detection in hostile environments. They also focus on minimizing noise, avoiding silhouetting, and blending into surroundings.
- Building a cohesive survival team involves assembling individuals with complementary skills, trust, and reliability, with continuous training, effective communication, and leadership flexibility being key to long-term survival.

9
PSYCHOLOGICAL PREPAREDNESS AND LEADERSHIP

Mental Resilience in Survival Situations

Mental resilience is not merely a beneficial trait but a crucial cornerstone of survival strategy in grid-down survival. Maintaining a positive outlook, managing stress effectively, and adapting to rapidly changing circumstances can significantly impact one's ability to navigate the challenges of a grid-down scenario. This section delves into the psychological aspects of survival, offering practical advice on cultivating mental resilience in the face of adversity.

First and foremost, understanding stress and its effects is vital. Stress, in survival situations, can be a double-edged sword. On one hand, it can heighten senses and improve reaction times, providing an edge in critical moments. On the other, prolonged stress can lead to mental fatigue, impaired decision-making, and a host of psychological issues, including anxiety and depression. Recognizing the signs of stress in oneself and others is the first step in managing it effectively. Deep breathing exercises, meditation, and routine maintenance can help mitigate stress and promote mental well-being.

Adaptability is another critical component of mental resilience. Adjusting to new challenges and unfamiliar environments is essential in a grid-down situation. This involves physical adaptation and a mental willingness to accept change and work with it rather than against it. Cultivating a mindset that views challenges as opportunities for growth rather than insurmountable obstacles can significantly enhance one's adaptability and overall resilience.

While it may seem counterintuitive in dire situations, optimism plays a critical role in survival. A positive outlook can boost morale for the individual and those around them, fostering a sense of hope and motivation to persevere. This does not mean ignoring the realities of the situation but instead choosing to focus on what can be controlled and finding solace in small victories and progress.

Building a solid support network is also crucial for maintaining mental resilience. In a grid-down scenario, isolation can quickly lead to despair. Sharing experiences, offering support, and working together towards common goals provide a sense of purpose and belonging, essential for psychological well-being. This sense of community can be a powerful antidote to the mental strain of survival situations.

Lastly, preparing mentally for a grid-down scenario can significantly improve one's resilience when faced with the actual event. This involves educating oneself about potential challenges and solutions and practicing mental and emotional coping strategies. Scenario planning, stress inoculation training, and mental rehearsal of survival situations can help build a psychological toolkit that is invaluable when reality strikes.

In conclusion, mental resilience in survival is a multifaceted discipline that encompasses stress management, adaptability, optimism, community building, and mental preparedness. Individuals can significantly improve their chances of surviving and thriving in adversity by cultivating these qualities and skills. As we discuss effective leadership and team dynamics, it's important to recognize that mental resilience is not just a personal asset but a foundational element of decisive leadership and cohesive team function in survival scenarios.

Effective Leadership and Team Dynamics

The importance of effective leadership and team dynamics cannot be overstated in a grid-down scenario. As individuals grapple with the psychological strain of survival, the role of a leader evolves into something far more critical than in ordinary circumstances. This section delves into the nuances of leadership and team dynamics in a survival context, offering practical advice for those in positions of responsibility.

Leadership in a grid-down situation is characterized by the ability to make decisions under pressure, inspire confidence among team members, and maintain a clear vision of survival and recovery. A leader's first task is to assess each team member's skills, strengths, and weaknesses, integrating these into a cohesive plan that leverages individual capabilities for the collective good. This assessment should be ongoing, as the survival stress can affect individuals' performance, and roles may need to be adjusted accordingly.

Communication is the linchpin of effective leadership and team dynamics. Leaders must establish open, honest, and clear channels of communication. This involves disseminating information and orders and listening to team members' concerns, suggestions, and feedback. In a survival situation, every team member's input can be valuable, and fostering a culture of mutual respect and inclusivity can significantly enhance group cohesion and morale.

Another critical aspect of leadership in survival scenarios is adaptability. Conditions can change rapidly, and leaders must be prepared to alter plans and strategies at a moment's notice. This flexibility should be balanced with a steady commitment to the group's overarching goals and the well-being of its members. Demonstrating resilience in the face of adversity can inspire the same in others, making adaptability a shared strength rather than a source of uncertainty.

Effective leaders also recognize the importance of maintaining morale. In the challenging environment of a grid-down scenario, hope can be as crucial as any physical resource. Leaders should find ways to motivate and uplift their team through shared goals, recognition of achievements, or maintaining a positive outlook. This does not mean ignoring the realities of the situation but instead framing challenges as obstacles that can be overcome together.

Finally, leadership in a survival context is not about authoritarian control but rather about fostering a sense of shared responsibility and empowerment. Leaders can cultivate a sense of ownership and investment in the group's success by involving team members in decision-making processes. This collaborative approach not only leverages the team's diverse skills and perspectives but also strengthens the social bonds that are essential for psychological resilience.

In conclusion, effective leadership and team dynamics in a grid-down survival scenario hinge on clear communication, adaptability, morale maintenance, and collaborative decision-making. Leaders who embody these principles can navigate survival challenges with a cohesive, motivated, and resilient team. As we move forward, resolving conflicts and negotiating effectively will become increasingly important, building on the foundation of strong leadership and team dynamics to ensure the group's continued survival and well-being.

Conflict Resolution and Negotiation

Resolving conflicts and effective negotiation are crucial for maintaining group cohesion and ensuring survival in a grid-down situation. Conflicts may arise from various sources, such as resource allocation, task distribution, personal grievances, or stress. Identifying the root cause is the first step in conflict resolution, which involves active listening and an empathetic understanding of each party's perspective.

Once the root causes are understood, establishing a resolution framework is necessary. This includes setting ground rules for respectful communication and focusing discussions on finding solutions rather than assigning blame. Reminding all parties of the common goal of survival and well-being can help diffuse tensions and encourage a collaborative approach.

Negotiation in a grid-down environment requires flexibility and creativity, as traditional bargaining may only sometimes be applicable. Interest-based negotiation can effectively address each party's underlying needs and interests. Techniques such as the "win-win" approach aim to find solutions that benefit all parties, requiring compromise but ensuring that core needs are met.

After reaching a resolution or agreement, it is crucial to implement it promptly and effectively. This involves defining the terms, assigning responsibilities, setting timelines, and conducting regular check-ins to ensure adherence and make necessary adjustments. A feedback mechanism and ongoing dialogue can prevent future conflicts and strengthen group dynamics.

Building a culture of collaboration and mutual respect within the group is essential. This can be achieved by resolving conflicts as they arise, preventing them through clear communication, equitable resource distribution, and fostering a sense of community. Regular group meetings to voice concerns, share ideas, and offer support are invaluable in maintaining this culture. In conclusion, mastering conflict resolution and negotiation is vital for navigating the challenges of a grid-down environment and maintaining group cohesion.

Stress Management Techniques

The psychological strain on individuals and groups can be immense in a grid-down scenario. If not managed properly, stress can undermine all survival survival efforts, leading to poor decision-making, conflict, and a breakdown in morale. Therefore, it is imperative that leaders and members of survival groups are equipped with effective stress management techniques to navigate these challenging times.

One of the first steps in managing stress is identifying and acknowledging its presence. Stress can manifest in various ways, including, but not limited to, physical symptoms such as headaches or fatigue, emotional symptoms like irritability or depression, and behavioral changes such as withdrawal or aggression. Recognizing these signs early on is crucial for addressing stress before it escalates.

Breathing exercises are a foundational tool in the stress management arsenal. Deep, controlled breathing can help calm the nervous system and reduce the physiological effects of stress. Techniques such as the 4-7-8 method, where you inhale for four seconds, hold your breath for seven seconds, and exhale for eight seconds, can be particularly effective. These exercises can be performed anywhere, anytime, making them an invaluable resource for immediate stress relief.

Physical activity is another vital stress management technique. Exercise improves physical health and has been shown to reduce anxiety and depression. Even in a grid-down scenario, simple activities like walking, stretching, or any form of manual labor can serve as effective stress relievers. The key is to integrate physical activity into daily routines to help maintain a level of normalcy and routine.

Mindfulness and meditation have gained recognition for reducing stress and improving overall well-being. Practicing mindfulness involves being fully present in the moment, aware of where we are and what we're doing, without being overly reactive or overwhelmed by what's happening around us. Guided meditations, focusing on a particular object, sound, or breath, can help achieve a calm state and reduce stress levels.

Journaling is another technique that can assist in

managing stress. Writing down thoughts and feelings can provide an outlet for expressing emotions, reflecting on experiences, and identifying stressors. This practice can help individuals process their emotions and gain perspective on their situation, contributing to better mental health.

Lastly, fostering a supportive community is essential for stress management. Sharing experiences, concerns, and coping strategies within a group can provide emotional support and strengthen collective resilience. Encouraging open communication and building trust within the group can help mitigate stress and promote a sense of unity and purpose.

In conclusion, stress management in a grid-down scenario requires a multifaceted approach that includes recognizing stress, employing physical and mental techniques to reduce its impact, and fostering a supportive community. By integrating these strategies into daily life, individuals and groups can better navigate the psychological challenges of survival situations, maintaining their focus, decision-making capabilities, and, ultimately, their hope for the future.

Building Morale and Maintaining Hope

A group's psychological landscape can swiftly become as challenging as physical hardships. Building morale and maintaining hope are not just supplementary tasks but essential to survival. This section delves into practical strategies for fostering a positive group dynamic and ensuring hope remains a steadfast companion, even in the darkest times.

Communication as a Cornerstone: Open, honest communication establishes trust and prevents the spread of rumors that can quickly erode morale. Leaders should encourage regular meetings where concerns, ideas, and feelings are freely expressed. This transparency helps create a sense of community and shared purpose, reinforcing the idea that everyone works together towards a common goal.

Setting Small, Achievable Goals: Setting and achieving small goals can provide a sense of progress and control in a situation where the future is uncertain. These accomplishments, whether building a shelter, securing a day's food, or simply maintaining a fire, can significantly boost morale. Celebrating these victories, no matter how minor they may seem, reinforces a positive outlook and the belief that survival and eventual recovery are possible.

Maintaining Routines and Traditions: Establishing routines can impart a sense of normalcy and structure, which is comforting during times of chaos. Similarly, preserving or adapting traditions, such as meal times, storytelling, or even birthdays, can strengthen bonds within the group and serve as reminders of the humanity and culture that survive despite the circumstances.

Encouraging Personal Time and Space: While group cohesion is vital, recognizing the importance of personal time and space is equally crucial. Individuals should be encouraged to spend time alone, engage in hobbies, or reflect. This can help mitigate feeling overwhelmed and provide a mental break from the stresses of survival.

Fostering a Culture of Learning and Adaptability: Encouraging the group to view the situation as an opportunity for learning and growth can transform challenges into valuable experiences. Sharing knowledge, skills, and even failures within the group enhances collective adaptability and reinforces the idea that every member has value and can contribute to the group's resilience.

Leading by Example: Leaders are critical in setting the tone for morale and hope. Even when faced with setbacks, demonstrating calmness, confidence, and compassion can inspire similar qualities in group members. Leaders should also be transparent about the challenges ahead but frame them in a way that emphasizes collective strength and the feasibility of overcoming obstacles together.

In conclusion, building morale and maintaining hope requires intention, effort, and creativity. They are about nurturing the human spirit as much as ensuring physical survival. By fostering a positive, cohesive group dynamic, leaders can help navigate the psychological complexities of a grid-down scenario, keeping despair at bay and paving the way for a resilient, hopeful community.

Training and Preparing Your Mind for Survival

During grid-down survival, the resilience of the human spirit is tested to its limits. Beyond the tangible necessities of food, water, and shelter lies the critical battlefield of the mind. Training and preparing your mind for survival is not just an option; it is necessary for those who aim to lead and thrive in the most challenging conditions.

The process of mental preparation for survival begins with understanding and acceptance. Acknowledge the potential severity of a grid-down scenario and its impacts on your life and community. This acceptance isn't about succumbing to fear but about recognizing the reality of the situation to better prepare for it. It's about building a mental framework that sees challenges as surmountable obstacles rather than insurmountable barriers.

Developing situational awareness is one of the first steps in training your mind for survival. This means being keenly aware of your environment and any changes, allowing you to anticipate problems and react swiftly and effectively. Regularly practice observing your surroundings, identifying potential threats, and imagining how you might deal with them. This exercise sharpens your awareness and enhances your ability to think on your feet—a crucial skill in any survival situation.

Another vital aspect of mental preparation is stress management. High-stress levels can cloud judgment, impair decision-making, and lead to panic—all detrimental in a survival scenario. Techniques such as deep breathing, meditation, and visualization can be powerful tools for maintaining a calm and clear mind. Regular practice of these techniques can help you develop the ability to stay composed under pressure, ensuring that you can make rational decisions when they matter most.

Resilience, the capacity to recover quickly from difficulties, is a trait that can be cultivated and strengthened over time. It involves maintaining a positive outlook, practicing gratitude, and embracing challenges as opportunities for growth. Encourage yourself and your team to view setbacks not as failures but as learning experiences. This mindset shift is pivotal in building the mental toughness required to navigate the uncertainties of a grid-down world.

Finally, leadership in such trying times hinges on inspiring and motivating others. A leader's confidence and calm demeanor can be contagious, helping to elevate the morale of the entire group. Therefore, part of your mental preparation should involve honing your communication skills and empathy. Listening actively, offering encouragement, and providing constructive feedback are all essential in fostering a cohesive and resilient team.

In conclusion, preparing your mind for survival is a multifaceted endeavor encompassing acceptance, situational awareness, stress management, resilience, and leadership. By dedicating time and effort to develop these mental skills, you equip yourself and those you lead with the psychological fortitude necessary to face the challenges of a grid-down scenario head-on. Remember, the body cannot go where the mind has not been. Therefore, let your mind venture into possibility, preparation, and unwavering resolve.

Chapter Summary

- Mental resilience is crucial in grid-down survival situations, involving stress management, adaptability, optimism, community building, and mental preparedness.
- Stress can sharpen senses and lead to mental fatigue; managing it involves recognizing signs, practicing deep breathing, meditation, and maintaining routines.
- Adaptability requires a mindset that views challenges as opportunities, emphasizing the importance of a positive outlook and building a solid support network.
- Preparing mentally for grid-down scenarios through education, scenario planning, and practicing coping strategies enhances resilience.
- Effective leadership in such scenarios involves decision-making under pressure, clear communication, fostering group cohesion, and maintaining morale.
- Conflict resolution and negotiation are essential for group cohesion. They focus on understanding root causes, establishing resolution frameworks, and implementing agreements fairly.
- Stress management techniques include: recognizing stress signs, engaging in physical

activity, practicing mindfulness, and fostering a supportive community.

- Building morale involves open communication, setting achievable goals, maintaining routines, encouraging adaptability, and leading by example to nurture hope and resilience.

10

COMMUNITY BUILDING AND NETWORKING

Forming and Strengthening Community Ties

In a grid-down scenario, society as we know it would undergo a fundamental transformation. The reliance on digital communication, centralized governance, and a cash-based economy would quickly become untenable. In such times, a community's strength and resilience would hinge on its members' ability to form and strengthen ties based on mutual support, trust, and cooperation.

Forming and strengthening community ties in a grid-down situation requires a proactive approach. Initially, it involves identifying individuals within your vicinity who share a common goal of survival and mutual aid. These could be neighbors, friends, or even acquaintances willing to prepare for or aware of the challenges posed by such scenarios. The foundation of these community ties is the understanding that collective efforts are more likely to yield positive outcomes in times of crisis than solitary endeavors.

Communication plays a pivotal role in this process. Communities must revert to more traditional means without the luxury of electronic communication. Establishing a system of regular face-to-face meetings, using notice boards in communal areas, or even setting up a system of messengers can ensure that information flows effectively within the group. These meetings and communications should focus on immediate survival strategies, long-term sustainability, and security.

Trust is another cornerstone of strong community ties. Building trust requires transparency, consistency, and reliability among members. Sharing skills, knowledge, and resources openly can foster a sense of belonging and mutual respect. Community members need to engage in activities that build relationships beyond the immediate survival needs, such as communal meals, joint training sessions on survival skills, or group projects to improve the collective living conditions.

The concept of mutual aid is essential in forming and strengthening community ties. This involves creating a system where resources are pooled, and skills are shared for the benefit of all members. For instance, those with medical knowledge could be responsible for health and wellness, while those with gardening or farming skills could lead food production efforts. The key is to identify and utilize the unique skills and resources each member brings to the table, ensuring that everyone has a role and feels valued within the community.

Adapting and overcoming challenges as a unified community can significantly increase the chances of surviving and thriving in a grid-down scenario. The process of forming and strengthening community ties is ongoing and evolves as the situation changes. It requires patience, empathy, and a shared commitment to a common cause. By laying the groundwork for solid community networks, individuals can create a resilient support system capable of withstanding the uncertainties of a post-grid world.

As communities solidify these ties, the next logical step in ensuring sustainability and self-sufficiency involves leveraging the diverse skills and resources within the group. This leads to establishing a bartering system and emphasizing trade skills, which become invaluable in a world where traditional currency and economic systems may no longer sway.

Bartering and Trade Skills

The conventional monetary system may falter in a grid-down scenario, rendering traditional currency less useful or obsolete. This shift necessitates a return to more primal exchange methods, primarily bartering and using trade skills. This section delves into the intricacies of these practices, offering practical advice on navigating and leveraging them for survival and community resilience.

Bartering, at its core, is the exchange of goods and services without the intermediary of money. In a grid-down situation, the value of items shifts dramatically, with practical, life-sustaining goods and services becoming highly prized. To engage effectively in bartering, one must first assess their resources and skills, identifying what they can offer. Simultaneously, understanding the needs and desires of your community is crucial. Items like food, water purification methods, medical supplies, and fuel often become highly sought after, but so do less obvious commodities like seeds, tools, and even knowledge or expertise in specific areas.

Developing trade skills is another vital aspect of surviving and thriving in a post-grid world. Skills that contribute directly to the sustenance and protection of a community become invaluable. These can range from agriculture, animal husbandry, and blacksmithing to more modern skills like solar panel installation and repair or radio communication expertise. Learning and mastering these skills ensures survival and enhances your value within a bartering system.

When engaging in barter, it's essential to establish and maintain trust within your community. Clear communication and transaction fairness help build a reputation as a reliable and honest trader, which can be invaluable in long-term survival scenarios. Additionally, understanding the basic principles of negotiation can help ensure that exchanges benefit all parties involved.

Moreover, the organization of bartering networks or

markets within a community can facilitate the efficient exchange of goods and services. These networks can range from informal agreements between neighbors to more structured gatherings at designated times and places. The key is ensuring these arrangements are secure, equitable, and accessible to all community members.

In conclusion, the revival of bartering and the emphasis on trade skills are survival strategies and opportunities to rebuild and strengthen community bonds. By fostering a culture of cooperation and mutual support, communities can more effectively navigate the challenges of a grid-down scenario, laying the foundation for a resilient and sustainable future.

Collaborative Survival Strategies

In a grid-down scenario, the importance of individual survival skills cannot be overstated. However, the true strength in enduring such challenging times often lies in a community's collective abilities and resources. Collaborative survival strategies are beneficial and essential for long-term sustainability and recovery, focusing on practical approaches and organizational structures that can enhance community resilience and mutual support during extended periods without the grid.

The first step in collaborative survival is forming alliances within your community based on mutual trust and the understanding that everyone has something valuable to contribute. It is crucial to identify individuals with essential skills—such as medical professionals, carpenters, and farmers. Organizing regular meetings to discuss plans, share knowledge, and distribute tasks helps create a comprehensive survival plan addressing food production, security, medical care, and communication.

One of the most effective ways to strengthen a community's survival capabilities is through skill-sharing workshops. These workshops can cover various topics, including first aid, food preservation, and basic carpentry. By leveraging the expertise within the community, members can learn from each other, reducing the community's overall vulnerability and ensuring that knowledge is continuously passed on.

In a grid-down situation, resources become exceedingly precious, making joint resource management essential to ensure equitable distribution of food, water, medicine, and fuel. Establishing a community store or bank where resources can be pooled and allocated according to need can prevent hoarding and conflict. This system requires transparent management and clear communication to maintain trust among community members.

Security becomes a paramount concern when the grid is down, and a community is more resilient to potential threats when it adopts a collective approach to defense. Organizing a neighborhood watch or a community patrol can deter threats and ensure the safety of all members. Training sessions on self-defense and discussions on non-violent conflict resolution should be part of the community's security strategy, along with establishing communication protocols for emergencies.

Access to hospitals and pharmacies is necessary for community health initiatives to become vital. Collaborating with medical professionals within the community to provide primary healthcare and emergency medical services is critical. Stockpiling essential medicines, organizing health education sessions, and creating natural remedies from locally available resources are all strategies that can improve the community's health resilience.

Collaborative survival strategies involve leveraging a community's collective strength and resources to withstand and recover from a grid-down scenario. By forming survival alliances, sharing skills, managing resources jointly, ensuring collective security, and prioritizing community health, a community can survive and lay the groundwork for rebuilding a sustainable way of life. The key to success lies in preparation, cooperation, and the willingness to support one another through the most challenging times.

Creating Mutual Aid Networks

As individuals, our ability to survive and thrive is significantly enhanced by forming strong, supportive networks. This is where the concept of creating mutual aid networks comes into play, serving as a cornerstone for resilient community building and networking. Mutual aid networks are collaborative structures that enable individuals and groups to pool resources, share skills, and support each other in times of need. This section delves into the practical steps for establishing these networks, ensuring they are effective, inclusive, and sustainable.

The first step in creating a mutual aid network is identifying potential members within your community who share a common interest in preparedness and resilience. This can include neighbors, friends, local businesses, and community organizations. The goal is to unite a diverse group of individuals with a wide range of skills, resources, and knowledge. Diversity in the network ensures a more comprehensive approach to problem-solving and resource allocation.

Once potential members have been identified, the next step is organizing an initial meeting to discuss the goals, expectations, and structure of the mutual aid network. This meeting is crucial for establishing trust, setting clear objectives, and determining each member's roles and responsibilities. It's important to create an environment of openness and inclusivity where every member feels valued and heard.

Effective communication is the backbone of any successful mutual aid network. Establishing reliable communication channels ensures members can coordinate efforts, share information, and provide support efficiently. These can include regular meetings, social media groups, email lists, or radio communication in more severe grid-down scenarios. The chosen methods should be accessible to all members and secure enough to protect the network's privacy and safety.

Resource pooling and skill sharing are fundamental aspects of mutual aid networks. Members can inventory their skills, tools, and resources, identifying what they can offer to the network and what they may need from others. These can range from practical skills like carpentry and gardening to resources like food, water, and medical supplies. The network can create a shared repository that enhances the community's collective resilience and self-sufficiency by pooling these resources.

Finally, it's essential to establish guidelines and protocols for how the network will operate during emergencies. This includes decision-making processes, resource allocation, and conflict resolution mechanisms. These guidelines ensure that the network can respond effectively and cohesively when faced with challenges.

Creating a mutual aid network is a proactive step towards building a resilient community capable of facing the uncertainties of a grid-down scenario. Individuals can enhance their ability to navigate such complexities through collaboration, shared resources, and mutual support. As we move forward, the principles of mutual aid can serve as a blueprint for fostering more robust, interconnected communities that are prepared to face any challenge together.

Legal and Ethical Considerations

In a grid-down scenario, society as we know it can be significantly altered. This brings the importance of community building and networking to the forefront. However, as we navigate these uncharted waters, we must remain vigilant about the legal and ethical considerations underpinning our actions and decisions. This awareness ensures that our efforts to rebuild and sustain communities are grounded in principles that promote fairness, respect, and dignity for all individuals involved.

Legal considerations in a grid-down scenario can be complex, given that existing laws can be temporarily unenforceable or subject to reinterpretation in emergency conditions. Despite these challenges, community leaders and members need to strive for adherence to the rule of law to the extent possible. This includes respecting property rights, upholding contractual obligations, and ensuring that any form of community governance or decision-making process is transparent and equitable. When the conventional legal system is not operational, communities may need to develop provisional codes of conduct or dispute resolution mechanisms, always with an eye toward eventual reintegration with broader societal norms.

Ethical considerations are equally paramount, as they guide our moral compass in times of crisis. The principles of beneficence (doing good), nonmaleficence (avoiding harm), autonomy (respecting individual freedom), and justice (ensuring fairness) become the cornerstones of community interactions. For instance, when establishing mutual aid networks, it is vital to ensure that resources are distributed based on need, without discrimination or favoritism. Similarly, decisions regarding community safety, resource allocation, and collaboration with neighboring groups must be made with a keen sense of ethical responsibility, recognizing the inherent worth of every community member.

Moreover, all community endeavors should emphasize transparency and accountability in the spirit of ethical conduct. This involves clear communication about the community's goals, challenges, and achievements and an openness to feedback and critique. By fostering an environment where ethical dilemmas are openly discussed and navigated collectively, communities can build a strong foundation of trust and mutual respect.

In navigating the legal and ethical landscapes of a grid-down scenario, we must consider the long-term implications of our actions. The decisions and precedents set during this period can have lasting effects on post-collapse communities' social fabric and governance structures. As such, a forward-thinking approach, coupled with a deep commitment to ethical principles and legal integrity, will be instrumental in laying the groundwork for resilient, just, and thriving communities in the aftermath of a crisis.

In conclusion, while the challenges of community building and networking in a grid-down scenario are manifold, they also present an opportunity to reaffirm our commitment to legal and ethical standards. By upholding these values, we not only navigate the immediate crisis with integrity but also contribute to creating a robust framework for the sustainable development of communities in a post-collapse world.

Chapter Summary

- In a grid-down scenario, communities must form and strengthen ties based on mutual support, trust, and cooperation, moving away from reliance on digital communication and centralized governance.
- Effective communication is crucial, requiring communities to use traditional means like face-to-face meetings and notice boards to ensure information flow.
- Trust and mutual aid are foundational, with community members sharing skills, knowledge, and resources and engaging in activities that build relationships beyond survival needs.
- Bartering and trade skills become essential as traditional currency may lose value; practical goods and services are highly prized, and trade skills directly contributing to community sustenance are invaluable.
- Collaborative survival strategies, including forming survival alliances, skill-sharing

workshops, joint resource management, and collective defense, are essential for long-term sustainability and recovery.

- Creating mutual aid networks involves identifying community members with shared interests in preparedness, organizing meetings to set goals and roles, and establishing effective communication and resource pooling.
- Legal and ethical considerations remain essential, with communities striving to adhere to the rule of law and ethical principles like fairness and respect, even when conventional legal systems are not operational.
- Rebuilding and sustaining communities post-collapse requires effective communication, resource management, security measures, education and skill-sharing, healthcare provision, and establishing governance and leadership structures.

11

LONG-TERM SUSTAINABILITY AND SELF-SUFFICIENCY

Sustainable Agriculture and Permaculture

A pivotal component of long-term sustainability and self-sufficiency is the establishment of sustainable agriculture and the principles of permaculture. This approach ensures food security in a grid-down scenario and promotes ecological health and resilience. The foundation of sustainable agriculture and permaculture lies in understanding and working with natural ecosystems rather than against them. This section delves into practical strategies and techniques to implement these concepts effectively.

To begin with, sustainable agriculture focuses on producing food, fiber, and other plant or animal products using farming techniques that protect the environment, public health, human communities, and animal welfare. This form of agriculture enables us to produce healthy food without compromising future generations' ability to do the same. The key practices include crop rotation, which helps prevent soil depletion and pest buildup; organic farming, which avoids synthetic pesticides and fertilizers; and agroforestry, which integrates trees and shrubs into agricultural landscapes.

On the other hand, permaculture is a design system for creating sustainable human habitats by following nature's patterns. It involves creating a diversified, resilient ecosystem that mimics the dynamics observed in natural ecosystems. Permaculture principles include observing and interacting with the natural environment to design efficient systems, capturing and storing energy, obtaining a yield, and applying self-regulation and feedback. These principles guide the design of sustainable homesteads, where water harvesting, waste recycling, and energy efficiency are seamlessly integrated.

Soil health is one of the most critical aspects of implementing sustainable agriculture and permaculture. Healthy soil is the foundation of a productive garden or farm. Techniques such as composting, mulching, and no-till farming can improve soil structure, enhance microbial activity, and increase water retention. Composting organic waste creates a nutrient-rich soil amendment, reducing the need for chemical fertilizers. Mulching helps suppress weeds, conserve soil moisture, and prevent soil erosion. No-till farming avoids soil disturbance, preserves soil structure, conserves water, and builds organic matter.

Water management is another vital component. Efficient

water use can be achieved through rainwater harvesting, drip irrigation, and the construction of swales and ponds to capture and store water in the landscape. These practices ensure that crops receive adequate water without wasting this precious resource.

Diversity is a hallmark of sustainable agriculture and permaculture. A diverse farm or garden is more resilient to pests, diseases, and weather fluctuations. Integrating a variety of crops, along with animals, beneficial insects, and native plants, creates a balanced ecosystem that supports itself. Crop rotation and intercropping (growing complementary plants together) can also improve yields and reduce pest problems.

Finally, integrating animals into the farm or garden ecosystem can provide multiple benefits. Chickens, for example, can offer natural pest control, manure for compost, and eggs. Bees can improve pollination, enhancing fruit and vegetable yields. The key is to create a symbiotic relationship between plants, animals, and humans, where each component supports and benefits the others.

In conclusion, sustainable agriculture and permaculture are not just farming practices but a philosophy of coexistence with nature. By adopting these practices, individuals and communities can build resilient, productive systems that meet their needs while enhancing the natural environment. This approach to food production and land management is crucial for navigating the challenges of a grid-down scenario, ensuring long-term sustainability and self-sufficiency.

Waste Management and Recycling

Managing waste and embracing recycling practices are crucial for long-term sustainability and self-sufficiency, especially without municipal waste services. Individuals and communities must adopt strategies that minimize waste production and repurpose materials whenever possible. This approach ensures health, safety, and resource conservation in a grid-down environment.

Effective waste management begins with segregation. It is essential to differentiate between organic waste, recyclables, and non-recyclable waste. Organic waste like food scraps and yard waste can be composted to create valuable fertilizer for gardens, thus closing the nutrient loop. At the same time, recyclables such as certain plastics, metals, glass, and paper should be cleaned and stored separately for repurposing.

Composting is a cornerstone of waste management in a grid-down scenario, allowing the conversion of organic waste into rich soil to enhance garden productivity. A simple compost pile or bin can be established with minimal effort, and maintaining a balance between nitrogen-rich materials and carbon-rich materials, along with regular turning, accelerates decomposition.

Recycling and repurposing materials extend their lifecycle and reduce the need for new resources. While melting down metals, glass, and certain plastics requires specific skills and equipment, repurposing or "upcycling" items is more accessible. For example, empty containers can be used for storage, and old clothing can be transformed into quilts or rags.

Reducing waste at the source is an effective strategy in a grid-down scenario. This involves mindful consumption and prioritizing durable, reusable products. Repairing broken items, choosing products with minimal packaging, and adopting a minimalist lifestyle can significantly reduce waste output.

Proper disposal of non-recyclable waste and hazardous materials is critical to prevent pollution and disease. Small landfills or incineration may be necessary in the absence of municipal services. Still, these methods must be cautiously approached to avoid contaminating water sources or creating health hazards. Regular cleaning and disinfection of waste storage areas help prevent pest infestations and maintain sanitary conditions.

Community initiatives enhance waste management and recycling efforts. Organizing community clean-up days, establishing shared composting facilities, and pooling resources for recycling projects can improve efficiency and foster a sense of solidarity. Education and awareness campaigns are also vital in promoting sustainable waste practices within the community.

In conclusion, effective waste management and recycling are critical components of living sustainably in a grid-down scenario. By adopting practices that reduce, reuse, and recycle waste, individuals and communities can mitigate environmental impact, conserve resources, and maintain health and safety standards. As we transition to discussing building and maintaining infrastructure, the principles of sustainability and resourcefulness continue to guide our approach to creating resilient, self-sufficient communities in the face of adversity.

Building and Maintaining Infrastructure

The importance of building and maintaining robust infrastructure cannot be overstated in the journey toward long-term sustainability and self-sufficiency, especially in scenarios where the grid has gone down. This infrastructure is not just about the physical constructs but also the systems and processes supporting a resilient and self-sufficient community.

The first step in building adequate infrastructure is to assess the community's needs. This involves identifying critical systems such as water supply, food production, shelter, and energy. Each system requires a different approach, but the overarching goal is to ensure they are resilient, sustainable, and independent from external inputs.

Water supply, for instance, can be secured through the collection and purification of rainwater, the digging of wells, or the development of spring-fed water systems. Each method has its advantages and challenges, but the key is to establish a reliable system that can be maintained with the resources and skills available within the community.

Food production is another critical area. Developing sustainable agriculture practices, such as permaculture, can help ensure a steady food supply. This involves not just cultivating crops but also integrating livestock, recycling nutrients, and conserving water. Community gardens and cooperative farming can also play a significant role in enhancing food security.

Shelter is about more than just building homes. It's about creating energy-efficient, durable structures made from locally sourced or recycled materials. Techniques such as earthbag construction, straw bale building, and the use of cob can be effective in many environments. Moreover, the design of living spaces should consider the efficient use of energy, with passive solar design and incorporating renewable energy systems being key considerations.

Energy infrastructure is one of the most challenging to address post-grid. However, developing microgrids, solar panels, wind turbines, and small-scale hydroelectric systems can provide sustainable energy solutions. The key is to design these systems for scalability and flexibility, allowing them to grow or change as the community's needs evolve.

Infrastructure maintenance is as critical as its construction. This involves regular checks and repairs, as well as a proactive approach to managing resources. It also requires the development of skills within the community, ensuring that there are individuals capable of repairing, improving, and innovating as needs and technologies change.

In conclusion, building and maintaining infrastructure in

a grid-down scenario is about more than just survival. It's about creating a foundation for a sustainable, self-sufficient community that can thrive in the long term. This requires careful planning, a commitment to sustainability, and a willingness to learn and adapt. By focusing on the essentials of water, food, shelter, and energy and ensuring that these systems are well-maintained, communities can build a resilient infrastructure supporting a high quality of life even in challenging circumstances.

Education and Skill Sharing for Self-Sufficiency

Communities striving for long-term survival and prosperity focus on transferring knowledge and skills among all members. This approach emphasizes practical education and skill sharing tailored to self-sufficiency, covering agriculture, carpentry, mechanical repair, and medical care. The aim is to equip every community member with diverse skills to enhance flexibility and resilience.

Skill sharing is facilitated through workshops, mentorship programs, and hands-on projects. Workshops target specific skills like water purification or solar panel construction. Mentorship programs allow for personalized learning under the guidance of experienced individuals. Hands-on projects provide practical learning experiences and contribute directly to community infrastructure.

However, implementing these educational initiatives can be challenging due to needing more resources, varying participant skill levels, and the need to juggle educational activities with daily survival tasks. Communities can address these challenges by being resourceful, creating teaching materials, tailoring classes to accommodate different skill levels, and integrating learning with essential daily activities.

Children and youth are vital to the community's future sustainability. By involving them in practical, hands-on learning, they become equipped to contribute meaningfully to the community while developing a strong sense of responsibility and belonging. This early engagement helps integrate education seamlessly into their everyday lives.

The dynamic nature of a grid-down scenario necessitates continuous learning and adaptability. Communities should cultivate an environment that encourages questioning, experimenting, and innovating to adapt to changing circumstances. This continuous improvement culture helps the community survive, thrive, and evolve.

In conclusion, effective education and skill sharing are the foundations of a resilient, self-sufficient community in a grid-down scenario. By focusing on practical skills, structuring educational programs effectively, and promoting an adaptive learning environment, communities can ensure their resilience and continued prosperity. This strategic focus on education empowers individuals to meet their needs while collectively strengthening the community.

Chapter Summary

- Sustainable agriculture, including permaculture, focuses on long-term ecological health and food security using crop rotation and agroforestry methods.
- Permaculture uses natural ecosystem principles to create sustainable habitats, emphasizing diversity and energy efficiency.
- Soil health is enhanced by composting, mulching, and no-till farming to improve fertility.
- Efficient water management techniques include rainwater harvesting and drip irrigation to ensure adequate supply without waste.
- Renewable energy sources like solar, wind, and micro-hydro are crucial for self-sufficiency and energy conservation, especially in off-grid scenarios.
- Water conservation is vital, involving efficient use and purification techniques to secure a dependable water supply.
- Waste management in off-grid situations involves segregation, composting, and repurposing to reduce environmental impact.
- Community resilience relies on building infrastructure and promoting education and skill sharing for adaptation and self-sufficiency.

12

ADAPTING TO A NEW WORLD

Embracing Change and Overcoming Challenges

In a grid-down scenario, adapting to the new world requires resilience and a profound willingness to embrace change and overcome the challenges that arise. This adaptation journey is not merely about survival but redefining our relationship with the environment, our communities, and the very essence of day-to-day living.

The initial shock of finding ourselves in a situation where the conveniences and supports of modern infrastructure are stripped away can be overwhelming. However, it's crucial to recognize that within this crisis lies an opportunity for profound personal growth and community strengthening. Embracing change in this context means acknowledging the loss of what was once familiar while being open to the possibilities of forging a new path.

One of the first steps in this journey is to assess our immediate environment and resources with fresh eyes. What was once taken for granted may now be a critical asset. For example, natural water sources, previously overlooked in favor of tap water, have become invaluable. Similarly, understanding local flora and fauna can transform from a hobbyist's interest to a vital skill in foraging for food and medicinal plants.

Overcoming challenges in a grid-down world also demands a shift in mindset from individualism to collective survival. The strength of a community can often be the deciding factor between merely surviving and truly thriving. Sharing skills, resources, and responsibilities becomes not just beneficial but essential. Those with knowledge in first aid, gardening, mechanical repair, or construction find their skills in high demand, and teaching others these skills helps to build a more resilient community.

Innovation plays a key role in adapting to this new world. Without access to conventional tools and materials, improvisation becomes a critical skill. The ability to repurpose materials or devise new methods for old tasks can significantly improve quality of life. For instance, creating a gravity-fed water filtration system from salvaged materials or developing a community barter system to distribute goods and services evenly.

Mental and emotional resilience are equally important. The stress and uncertainty of a grid-down scenario can take a toll on even the most robust individuals. Cultivating a mindset that focuses on solutions rather than problems, finds joy in small victories, and maintains hope and positivity in the face of adversity is crucial. When shared within a community, this mental resilience creates an atmosphere of mutual support and encouragement that can weather the most challenging times.

As we navigate the challenges of adapting to a grid-down world, we must remember that our greatest resource is our collective human spirit. By embracing change, fostering community, innovating solutions, and maintaining resilience, we can survive and build a foundation for a new way of living that could redefine our future for the better.

Innovative Problem Solving

Thinking outside the box is a critical survival skill. The world as we know it transforms, and with it, our daily challenges. This section delves into the essence of innovative problem-solving, a skill that not only aids in adapting to new circumstances but also in thriving amidst them.

Innovative problem-solving in a post-grid world involves creativity, practicality, and resourcefulness. It's about looking at what you have through a different lens and imagining how it can serve a purpose it was never intended for. This mindset shift is vital for overcoming challenges when traditional systems and supports are no longer available.

One of the first steps in cultivating this skill is to assess your environment and resources with fresh eyes. Everything around you has potential. For instance, consider the natural resources at your disposal. A fallen tree isn't just an obstacle; it's a source of firewood, a potential shelter structure, or even raw material for tools and utensils. Similarly, an abandoned vehicle can be a source of metal, glass, and other materials that can be repurposed in countless ways.

Another aspect of innovative problem-solving is the ability to improvise. This means using available materials and knowledge to create solutions on the fly. For example, if you're facing a water purification challenge, understanding the basics of filtration and disinfection can help you devise a makeshift purification system using charcoal, sand, and sunlight. This improvisational skill hinges on a solid foundation of knowledge across various domains, highlighting the importance of a well-rounded skill set in survival situations.

Collaboration plays a significant role in innovative problem-solving. Pooling knowledge and skills with others broadens the range of potential solutions and fosters a sense of community and mutual support, which is invaluable in challenging times. Through collaboration, individuals can combine their strengths and compensate for each other's weaknesses, leading to more effective and sustainable solutions.

Finally, embracing a mindset of continuous learning and adaptation is essential. The post-grid world is dynamic, with new challenges and opportunities emerging regularly. Staying curious, open to new ideas, and willing to experiment can lead to discoveries that significantly improve your quality of life in a grid-down scenario.

In conclusion, innovative problem-solving is a multifaceted skill encompassing creativity, improvisation, collaboration, and continuous learning. By developing this skill, individuals can better navigate the uncertainties of a post-grid world, turning challenges into opportunities for growth and innovation. As we move forward, the role of technology in this new landscape will be a critical factor to consider, offering both challenges and solutions in our journey of adaptation.

The Role of Technology in a Post-Grid World

The collapse of the power grid and the subsequent failure of conventional communication, transportation, and utility infrastructures compel us to reassess our relationship with technology. This section delves into how we can adapt and leverage technology in a post-grid world, ensuring our survival and facilitating the rebuilding of society.

Initially, it's crucial to understand that not all technology is rendered obsolete in the absence of a power grid. Solar panels, wind turbines, and other renewable energy sources become invaluable assets. These technologies can power essential devices, from communication tools to medical equipment, providing a lifeline in the aftermath of a grid collapse. Adaptation involves the use of these technologies and the knowledge to maintain and repair them. Community workshops and shared knowledge bases become critical for preserving these skills.

Communication technology, in particular, is undergoing a significant shift. Without the internet and cellular networks, alternative forms of communication, such as shortwave radios and satellite phones, gain prominence. These tools enable communities to stay informed, share resources, and coordinate recovery efforts. The knowledge of operating these devices, often overlooked in a grid-dependent world, becomes a vital skill set.

Moreover, the role of technology in purifying and managing water supplies cannot be overstated. Simple yet effective technological solutions like solar water disinfection (SODIS) methods and manually operated water purifiers ensure access to clean water, a critical component of survival. The innovation lies in adapting these technologies to local conditions and materials available, underscoring the importance of ingenuity in a post-grid world.

Agriculture and food production also see a technological transformation. Techniques such as permaculture, aquaponics, and vertical farming, powered by renewable energy sources, offer sustainable ways to produce food. These methods not only ensure food security but also contribute to the regeneration of the ecosystem. The knowledge of these technologies and traditional farming practices form the backbone of a resilient food system.

In healthcare, technology plays a pivotal role in maintaining community health. Portable diagnostic tools powered by renewable energy enable the monitoring of health conditions, while telemedicine practices, adapted to work over radio or other basic communication networks, allow for the sharing of medical knowledge and advice. Creating and distributing essential medicines and treatments, relying on modern and traditional methods, has become a community-driven effort.

Adapting to a new world where technology must be reimagined and repurposed is challenging. It requires a shift in mindset from consumption to conservation, from dependence to self-sufficiency. The resilience of technology in a post-grid world lies not in its complexity but in its adaptability and the community's ability to innovate and preserve knowledge. This transition ensures survival and lays the foundation for a future where technology, powered by renewable energy and driven by community needs, plays a central role in rebuilding and enhancing society.

Preserving Knowledge and Culture

In a grid-down scenario, where modern technology and conveniences are inaccessible, preserving knowledge and culture is crucial. The loss of digital infrastructure would significantly impact access to knowledge, making it essential to prioritize the preservation of physical books, documents, and other educational materials. Establishing community libraries or archives can serve as central points for knowledge storage and sharing, focusing on a wide range of subjects such as agriculture, medicine, engineering, and history to ensure a well-rounded knowledge base is available.

Workshops and apprenticeships should also encourage and document the practice of traditional skills and crafts. These can facilitate the transfer of practical knowledge from basic carpentry and metalwork to more complex skills like weaving and pottery. Such skills preserve cultural heritage and provide communities with the means to rebuild and sustain themselves without relying on modern industrial processes.

Culture, encompassing language, art, traditions, and social practices, is the soul of a community, and its preservation becomes a communal effort in a world without the grid. Oral traditions, such as storytelling, songs, and folklore, play a vital role in passing down history, moral lessons, and cultural identity from one generation to the next. Additionally, creating and maintaining physical records of cultural practices, including written records, drawings, paintings, and other forms of art that depict cultural events, traditional clothing, and architecture, is essential. Encouraging the continued practice of cultural festivals and ceremonies can help maintain a sense of community and continuity.

Education will be the cornerstone of preserving knowledge and culture, requiring communities to adopt more flexible and adaptive forms of education. This might include community-led classes, mentorship programs, and practical, hands-on learning experiences directly relevant to life in a post-grid world. In this context, everyone has something to teach and something to learn, making sharing knowledge across generations a communal responsibility, with elders passing down wisdom and younger members contributing fresh ideas and innovations.

Preserving knowledge and culture in a post-grid scenario is not merely about survival; it's about ensuring that the essence of who we are as a species is not lost. By proactively safeguarding our collective knowledge and cultural heritage, communities can lay the foundation for a resilient, sustainable future where the human spirit thrives even in the face of adversity. This endeavor will aid in the practical aspects of rebuilding society and ensure that the richness of human culture continues to inspire and guide future generations.

Environmental Stewardship

The immediate aftermath of a grid-down scenario may have us focused on survival, but as we adapt to a new world, environmental stewardship becomes not just a moral imperative but a practical necessity. This section delves into the principles and practices of sustaining and nurturing the environment in times of crisis, ensuring that our survival strategies are aligned with the health of our planet.

The cornerstone of environmental stewardship in a grid-down world is the sustainable management of resources. Water, soil, and air—the essential elements of life—must be protected and preserved with utmost care. Water conservation becomes critical; methods such as rainwater harvesting, dew collection, and greywater recycling for agricultural purposes should be implemented. Soil health can be maintained through composting, crop rotation, and avoiding chemical fertilizers, which may be scarce or unavailable. Air quality, though less immediately controllable, benefits from reducing industrial pollutants and carefully managing biomass burning.

Biodiversity is another critical aspect of environmental stewardship. A grid-down scenario likely disrupts ecosystems, making protecting native species and habitats more important than ever. Establishing and maintaining seed banks ensures the preservation of plant diversity, which is crucial for food security and ecological balance. Similarly, protecting wildlife by avoiding overhunting and preserving natural habitats helps maintain the balance of ecosystems upon which human survival ultimately depends.

Renewable energy sources become invaluable in a world without the grid. Solar, wind, and hydropower can provide sustainable energy solutions, reducing our dependence on fossil fuels and minimizing our ecological footprint. Implementing renewable energy systems not only addresses immediate energy needs but also sets a foundation for the long-term sustainability of communities.

Waste management is transformed in a grid-down scenario. Communities must adopt zero-waste practices without the infrastructure for waste collection and disposal.

This involves the reduction of waste production, the reuse of materials, and the recycling or composting of organic and inorganic waste. Such practices reduce environmental impact and turn waste into valuable resources.

Finally, environmental education plays a pivotal role in sustaining these efforts. Knowledge about sustainable living practices passed down through generations, becomes a cornerstone of community resilience. Workshops, hands-on demonstrations, and community projects can foster a culture of environmental stewardship, ensuring that sustainability principles are ingrained in the fabric of society.

In adapting to a new world, our survival is intricately linked to the health of our environment. By embracing the principles of environmental stewardship, we ensure our immediate survival and lay the groundwork for a sustainable future. This holistic approach to living in harmony with our planet is not just a strategy for survival; it is a testament to our resilience and commitment to preserving the world for future generations.

Chapter Summary

- Adapting to a grid-down world involves embracing change, assessing resources anew, and fostering community strength.
- Overcoming challenges requires shifting from individualism to collective survival, sharing skills, and innovating solutions.

- Mental and emotional resilience, focusing on solutions, and maintaining positivity are crucial in a grid-down scenario.
- Innovative problem-solving is key, involving creativity, practicality, resourcefulness, and collaboration.
- Technology plays a transformative role, with renewable energy sources and alternative communication methods becoming vital.
- Preserving knowledge and culture through community libraries, traditional skills workshops, and education ensures continuity for future generations.
- Environmental stewardship is essential, focusing on sustainable resource management, biodiversity protection, and renewable energy.
- Planning for future generations emphasizes education in practical skills, healthcare knowledge, and building resilient communities.

THE PATH FORWARD

Reflecting on Lessons Learned

As we navigate the closing pages of our journey through the uncharted territories of a world without the grid, it becomes imperative to pause and reflect on the myriad lessons that have emerged from the shadows of this new reality. The transition from a life of convenience and instant connectivity to one of self-reliance and resilience has not been without its trials. Yet, within these challenges lie invaluable insights that prepare us for a future of uncertainties and enrich our understanding of what it means to persevere truly.

One of the most profound lessons learned is the undeniable importance of preparedness. The initial shock accompanying the loss of the grid serves as a stark reminder of the fragility of our modern infrastructure. It underscores the necessity of having a well-thought-out plan that encompasses not just the immediate needs of survival, such as water, food, and shelter, but also long-term sustainability through skills like gardening, foraging, and renewable energy sources. The journey from dependence to independence is paved with the knowledge and skills acquired before necessity becomes the master.

Adaptability, too, has proven to be a cornerstone of surviving and thriving in a grid-down scenario. The ability to adjust to new challenges, innovate with the resources at hand, and abandon preconceived notions of living is crucial. This adaptability extends beyond the physical to the psychological, where mental resilience becomes just as important as any survival skill. The capacity to maintain hope, find joy in simplicity, and persevere through adversity ultimately defines the human spirit in the face of collapse.

Equally important is the lesson of self-sufficiency, yet it is within this lesson that a paradox emerges. While the initial focus may be on individual or familial survival, it becomes increasingly clear that true self-sufficiency is intertwined with the community's well-being. Individuals' skills, resources, and strengths can be pooled to create a collective resilience far greater than the sum of its parts. Through this synergy, the foundation for a sustainable future is laid, one where mutual aid and cooperation become the pillars of a new society.

Reflecting on these lessons, it is evident that the path forward is not one of isolation but of connection. The challenges faced in a world without the grid have illuminated the intrinsic value of community, the strength derived from shared hardship, and the profound impact of collective action. As we stand at the threshold of this new world, this spirit of collaboration and unity will light the way.

The Importance of Community and Collaboration

In a grid-down scenario, the significance of individual preparedness cannot be overstated. However, as we have navigated through the complexities and challenges of surviving without our usual infrastructures, one truth has emerged with undeniable clarity: the importance of community and collaboration. This realization is a byproduct of hardship and a fundamental principle that can guide us toward a more resilient future.

The concept of self-sufficiency is often romanticized, conjuring images of a lone survivor braving the elements with nothing but their wits and willpower. While individual skills and preparedness are crucial, they are but one piece of the survival puzzle. Humans are inherently social beings; our strength lies in our ability to work together, share knowledge, and support each other through adversity.

Community and collaboration offer several advantages in a grid-down situation. Firstly, they allow for the pooling of resources. When individuals come together, they can combine their supplies, leading to a more efficient use of resources and reducing the risk of shortages. This pooling is not limited to physical resources but extends to skills and knowledge. In a community, individuals can specialize in certain tasks, leading to more efficient work and better outcomes.

Secondly, collaboration enhances security. In times of crisis, threats can come from environmental challenges, scarcity of resources, or even other people. A community can organize collective defense measures, create warning systems, and establish protocols that a single individual or a small family unit would struggle to implement independently.

Moreover, the psychological benefits of being part of a community cannot be overlooked. The stress and mental strain of surviving a grid-down scenario can be overwhelming. A support network provides emotional comfort and can be critical to maintaining mental health and resilience.

However, building and maintaining a community in such challenging times has its challenges. It requires trust, communication, and a willingness to put the group's needs alongside, if not before, individual desires. Leadership and decision-making become more complex but also more critical. Establishing clear roles, responsibilities, and rules can help manage these challenges.

As we look toward the future, the lessons learned about the value of community and collaboration should be remembered. These principles should be integrated into our preparedness plans from the outset. Building strong, supportive networks now, based on mutual aid and respect, can significantly enhance our collective resilience in the face of future crises.

In conclusion, while individual preparedness is essential, the power of community and collaboration stands out as a beacon of hope and strength. By fostering these relationships and networks, we increase our chances of survival in a grid-down scenario and pave the way for a more connected and resilient society. As we move forward, let us carry with us the understanding that together, we are stronger, and it is through collaboration that we can build a path to a more secure and sustainable future.

Continued Learning and Adaptation

Understanding the pivotal role that community and collaboration play in navigating the challenges of a grid-down scenario, it becomes evident that our journey does not end with merely establishing connections and fostering teamwork. The essence of truly thriving in such situations lies in our ability to engage in continued learning and adaptation. This process is not just about acquiring new skills or knowledge but about evolving our mindset to be more resilient, resourceful, and responsive to the changing dynamics of our environment.

Continued learning encompasses a broad spectrum of activities in the context of grid-down survival. It involves staying informed about the latest survival techniques, understanding the advancements in sustainable living practices, and keeping abreast of the developments in renewable energy sources. This knowledge enhances our ability to sustain ourselves without the grid and empowers us to make informed decisions that can significantly improve our quality of life in such circumstances.

Moreover, adaptation is a critical component of this learning process. It's about taking the knowledge we've acquired and applying it to our unique situations. This might mean modifying a solar panel setup to work more efficiently in your specific geographic location or adapting a water purification technique to better suit your resources. The key is to be flexible and open to experimenting with different solutions to find what works best for your community and environment.

This journey of continued learning and adaptation also involves significant trial and error. Only some ideas will be successful, and only some plans will unfold as expected. However, each attempt, whether successful or not, is a valuable learning experience that contributes to our collective knowledge pool. Sharing these experiences with the community helps refine our strategies and strengthens the bonds within the community, as everyone benefits from the shared wisdom.

Embracing a mindset of continued learning and adaptation also means being proactive in seeking new information and growth opportunities. This could involve participating in workshops, joining online forums, or organizing community learning events. The goal is to create a culture of continuous improvement, where everyone is encouraged to share their knowledge and experiences for the betterment of the community.

In conclusion, as we navigate the path forward in a grid-down world, continued learning and adaptation principles stand as beacons of hope. They remind us that our ability to thrive in such scenarios is not fixed but is an ever-evolving process that requires dedication, curiosity, and a willingness to embrace change. By committing to this journey of continuous growth, we not only enhance our chances of survival but also pave the way for a future where we can live in harmony with our environment, resilient and self-sufficient, regardless of the challenges we may face.

Staying Prepared for Future Uncertainties

Understanding the importance of staying prepared for future uncertainties is paramount in preparing for grid-down scenarios. This mindset does not merely involve accumulating supplies or mastering survival skills; it encompasses a holistic approach to readiness that evolves with time and the changing nature of threats.

First and foremost, it is crucial to maintain a vigilant watch on the world's socio-economic and environmental trends. The nature of threats is ever-changing, and what may seem like a distant concern today could become a pressing reality tomorrow. Regularly updating your knowledge base through credible news sources, scientific reports, and community insights can provide early warnings of emerging risks.

Equally important is the practice of scenario planning. This involves considering potential future events, no matter how unlikely they may seem, and considering how they could impact your preparedness strategy. By doing so, you can identify gaps in your current plan and adjust accordingly. This might mean diversifying your food storage, learning new skills, or strengthening your community ties.

Another critical aspect of staying prepared is the continuous review and rotation of your supplies. Over time, stored food can expire, equipment can become obsolete, and personal needs can change. Regularly auditing your supplies ensures that everything you have stored remains useful and accessible when needed. This also allows you to test your gear and practice your skills, ensuring that both remain sharp and effective.

In addition to physical preparations, mental resilience plays a critical role in navigating future uncertainties. Cultivating a mindset that embraces adaptability, problem-solving, and calmness under pressure can significantly improve one's ability to respond effectively to unexpected challenges. This can be achieved through mental exercises, stress management techniques, and learning from past experiences.

Lastly, building and nurturing a community of like-minded individuals offers a support network that can be invaluable during times of crisis. Sharing knowledge, resources, and skills not only strengthens individual preparedness but also enhances the collective resilience of the community. This sense of solidarity and mutual aid is a powerful asset in facing future uncertainties.

In conclusion, staying prepared for future uncertainties requires a dynamic and proactive approach. It involves not just a well-stocked pantry or a set of survival skills but a comprehensive strategy that includes staying informed, scenario planning, continuous learning, mental resilience, and community building. By embracing these principles, you can confidently navigate the path forward, ready to face whatever challenges the future may hold.

Inspiring Others to Prepare

In the journey toward self-reliance and preparedness, one of the most profound steps we can take is to inspire others to embark on this path with us. A community's resilience during times of crisis is not solely dependent on the preparedness of individuals but on the collective preparedness of its members. As we have navigated through the intricacies of preparing for a grid-down scenario, extending this knowledge beyond our immediate circle is imperative, fostering a culture of preparedness that can withstand the tests of unforeseen challenges.

Inspiring others to prepare is not about instilling fear but sharing knowledge and experiences that empower and motivate. It begins within our families, extends to friends, and eventually permeates the wider community. Sharing stories from those who have experienced natural disasters or other emergencies can be a powerful catalyst for change. These narratives and practical advice and demonstrations can transform apathy into action.

Education plays a crucial role in this endeavor. Organizing workshops or informational sessions on basic survival skills, such as water purification, food storage, and first aid, can demystify the process of preparedness for many. These sessions can be held in community centers, schools, or online platforms, making them accessible to a broader audience. The key is to present this information in a manner that is engaging, practical, and devoid of sensationalism.

Moreover, leveraging social media and other digital platforms can amplify our reach, allowing us to share resources, tips, and personal experiences with a global audience. Blogs, podcasts, and video tutorials are excellent mediums for disseminating information on preparedness strategies, gear reviews, and survival skills. By creating informative, relatable, and actionable content, we can inspire a wave of preparedness that transcends geographical boundaries.

However, it is crucial to approach these efforts with empathy and understanding. The journey toward preparedness is personal and unique for each individual. Some may be motivated by personal experiences with adversity, while others may be driven by a desire to protect their loved ones. Recognizing these motivations and addressing the barriers that prevent people from taking action is essential. This may involve debunking myths about preparedness, offering cost-effective solutions, or simply providing a supportive community for individuals to share their concerns and achievements.

Inspiring others to prepare cannot be overstated as we look to the future. In a world fraught with uncertainties, our communities' collective preparedness is our strongest asset. By sharing our knowledge, experiences, and resources, we not only enhance our own resilience but also contribute to a more prepared and resilient society. This is the path forward—a journey not walked alone but together, with a shared vision of preparedness that safeguards our collective future.

Concluding Thoughts

As we draw this guide to a close, we must reflect on our journey together. From understanding the basics of survival in a grid-down scenario to mastering the skills necessary for long-term resilience, we've covered a broad spectrum of knowledge and strategies. The importance of preparation cannot be overstated, and by now, you should feel more equipped to face the uncertainties of a world without the conveniences of modern infrastructure.

However, the path forward requires more than just individual readiness. It demands a collective effort and a shared commitment to survive and thrive in the face of adversity. A community's resilience can significantly amplify the efforts of the individual, creating a network of support that can withstand the toughest challenges. Therefore, as you continue to hone your skills and expand your knowledge, consider how you can contribute to your community's resilience. Whether through sharing resources, offering training, or simply fostering a spirit of cooperation, your efforts can inspire others to prepare and create a stronger, more resilient society.

Remember, the goal of this guide is not to instill fear but to empower you with the knowledge and skills to confidently navigate a grid-down scenario. The journey doesn't end here; it evolves with each new skill learned, every piece of knowledge shared, and through every challenge faced with courage and determination. As you move forward, remember that preparation is an ongoing, lifelong commitment to ensuring the safety and well-being of yourself and those around you.

In conclusion, the path forward is continuous learning, adaptation, and community engagement. It's about building a survival kit and a survival mindset that embraces the challenges of a grid-down world as opportunities to grow, learn, and strengthen the bonds that tie us together. As you close this guide, remember that the most powerful tool at your disposal is not the gear you've acquired or the supplies you've stockpiled but the knowledge you've gained and the community you've built. Together, there is no challenge too great to overcome.

Your Feedback Matters

Thank you for joining me on this journey. If the book inspired you, please share your thoughts by leaving a review on Amazon using the QR code below. Your feedback is invaluable and helps guide others. I'm grateful for your time and hope the insights you've gained enrich your quest for knowledge.

ABOUT THE AUTHOR

Anthony Bennett is a passionate advocate for sustainable living and self-sufficiency. With a background in environmental science and years of hands-on experience in homesteading, his practical advice and innovative solutions for living off the land have inspired many to pursue a more sustainable and independent lifestyle. Through his "Self-Sufficient Living" series, including "How to Build the Perfect Backyard Homestead" and "How to Survive When the Grid Goes Down," Anthony shares his wealth of knowledge on creating resilient and productive homesteads. When he's not writing, Anthony tends to his homestead.

www.ingramcontent.com/pod-product-compliance
Lightning Source LLC
Chambersburg PA
CBHW052140070526
44585CB00017B/1903